All Six Legs

To Jolene
Briant Blessings

All Six Legs

Denise McLeod

Matador
9 Priory Business Park,
Wistow Road, Kibworth Beauchamp,
Leicestershire. LE8 0RX
Tel: 0116 279 2299
Email: books@troubador.co.uk
Web: www.troubador.co.uk/matador
Twitter: @matadorbooks

ISBN 978 1838591 083

British Library Cataloguing in Publication Data.
A catalogue record for this book is available from the British Library.

Printed and bound in the UK by TJ International, Padstow, Cornwall
Typeset in 11pt Aldine401 BT by Troubador Publishing Ltd, Leicester, UK

Matador is an imprint of Troubador Publishing Ltd

This book is dedicated to the memory of the most extraordinary dog I have ever known.

My best friend, my teacher, my inspiration and my protector.

Cloud.

My heart still aches for you.

Contents

Introduction

Hello and welcome to my second book, All Six Legs. I do hope that you enjoy it!

When I released my first book, A Dog Behaviourist's Diary, I was a mixture of angst and worry, excitement and hope. I had no idea how it would be received by readers or how the technique released within it, Turn and Face, would be accepted by the dog training world. I had so many sleepless nights I could hardly function the days before and just after, the release. I worried myself nearly to death.

But, as it turns out, I need not have worried at all. I have been simply overwhelmed by the positive response from readers of the book, so many kind and supportive messages have been received and so many positive reviews left. As for the worlds 'acceptance of' Turn and Face, well I will leave that explanation to the chapter about it, later in this book!

I could not have ever dreamed that the book would make such a wonderful impact and I have been truly humbled and honored to have received great feed-back from so many people and even some of the world's most well known dog trainers.

I would like to thank each and every one of the readers of that book, who wrote to me, left positive reviews, sent me videos of their dogs transformation and who continue to give me feedback about the beneficial effects that the book still has, on dogs worldwide. And I'd like to sincerely thank all of those who encouraged me to write this, my second book.

So here it is! All Six Legs continues in the same vein as A Dog Behaviourist's Diary. Once again, based on real cases, this book takes us on a journey into the lives of some very special dogs and their equally special owners. It explores the cases that became great learning points for me. Cases which changed the way I think about dogs and people. It also reveals some amazing and sometimes weird ways which people and dogs are connected, for the better of all.

Once again there is laughter and sadness, highs and lows. But overall the book is a celebration of what it is to be a human, that loves a dog. Or indeed a dog, that loves a human. This book even contains life saving information that might one day save the life of your dog! Or you!

Wherever possible, permission has been gained to share the details of the cases, but where it has not been possible, the names and some of the identifying details have been changed to preserve client confidentiality. But all of the behaviour specific information in this book, is real.

So it's time to grab yourself a cuppa, or a beer and find a comfy seat to sit down on and discover what makes the bonding of two legs, with four, so very, very special. I welcome you back into the world of All Six Legs.

May the love of a dog be with you, always.

Sally:
The Miracle of Dogs

When I answered the phone it was immediately clear that this was one very worried dog owner. Her voice was cautious, tentative, as if she were about to reveal a long-hidden secret that she had no wish to speak of. There was deep sadness, tinged with helplessness.

"Hello, I need your help with our dog. Our neighbour recommended you." There was a long pause before she continued, so I waited. She continued warily. "Our dog has started being aggressive to my daughter and it is breaking my daughter's heart and frightening me. It's making us both ill with worry." She sounded so desperate, almost haunted.

"Oh dear, I am so sorry to hear this," I replied. "Tell me, when did this begin, and what do you mean by aggression?"

"A few weeks back. They are, or were, the best of friends and Sally is a lovely dog in every way, but there seems no reason for this sudden aggression and I can't have her being aggressive to my daughter. She just started growling one day and she now growls every time she sees Jane. I am afraid that she will bite her and Jane is so upset, and she keeps crying, and…" she tailed off as she took a deep breath, "… and we just can't go on like this. Please can you help us?" The pain in her voice cut right through me; it was palpable and, it seems, contagious. I felt it in my own heart. Little

1

Karma, who had been sitting at my side having a cuddle, got up and crept off the sofa. Maybe she could feel it too?

Personally I don't consider growling to be aggression, more *an attempt to avoid aggression*. It is a signal that what a person is doing or about to do is making a dog uncomfortable. Sometimes a growl is justified; sometimes it is not. But this was not the time to share my viewpoint; I needed to listen to the worried lady and find out more details of the case.

★

Dogs that growl at children can do so for a variety of reasons, but because of the potentially serious consequences of such an action it is important that I see the dog and the child before jumping to any conclusions. As the lady continued I got nothing more in the way of clues, other than how desperate they were to understand and resolve the situation.

So I arranged to go to their home to met Sally and Jane for myself. As I set out that day I felt unsettled and worried. I had found out little from the phone conversation other than Sally the dog growled at Jane and that prior to this new behaviour, Sally and Jane had been the best of friends.

As I drove toward their home, I felt as gloomy as the weather that surrounded me. I very much hoped that I could get to the bottom of this case and help this lady, by encouraging what sounded like a very troubled daughter and otherwise lovely dog to find peace with one another again.

When I arrived at their door, I was greeted by a lot of barking. Once the door was opened a very friendly, lively little dog was jumping up at me in a very excited but amiable fashion. She wagged her tail madly and looked like a very sweet little thing, not at all like the snarling dog that I had imagined. The lady who met me at the door seemed as worried and anxious

2

as she had sounded on the phone, as well as looking very tired indeed.

She beckoned for me to come in and as I did my best to fend off the over-exuberance of the little dog, a Spaniel cross, I observed that I felt no threat at all from this bundle of happy furriness. I found it hard to imagine such a friendly dog growling at anyone – she certainly wasn't growling at me.

I was ushered into a living room. Once I had sat down the lady went off to make a cup of tea and I was left alone with Sally. Sally continued to wag her tail and tried to jump up on my knee for some more close attention. It seemed she was used to being on someone's knee. Gently, I tried to push her back onto the floor.

I glanced around the living room in search of clues while I waited. I observed on the mantelpiece above the fire a number of trophies and red rosettes. The lady owner returned with a cup of tea and as she did, Sally left my side and went to sit with her. The lady reached out and without thinking began to stroke Sally gently around her neck and ears. Sally pushed in toward the contact, her eyes half-closed, seemingly in pleasure at the lady's touch. What a delightful dog she seemed! This was a dog used to affection and an owner used to giving it.

We began to discuss the facts of the case. Sally had been bought by the lady for her daughter some eight years previously when the young girl's father had been tragically killed in a car crash whilst driving home from work one day. The child had sunk into a deep sadness when her father had been taken so unexpectedly and so the lady had decided to buy her a puppy, the puppy she had always longed for, to try to bring some happiness and focus back into her sad daughter's life.

The dog's arrival had had a transformative effect on the then five-year-old daughter who had thrown all her energy into playing with and training the little pup. She had taught Sally many tricks and played hide and seek with her. Later she had taken up agility and had gone to classes and then competitions with her. The woman pointed at the glass trophies and red rosettes, proudly displayed centre stage on the mantelpiece. Signs of an agility career of significant success! Her mother smiled for the first time as she beamed with pride at just how much Jane had achieved with Sally.

But then a year or so ago, Sally had started to slow down and knock poles off jumps. The vet had concluded that she had some arthritis and Jane had decided that it was not fair to take Sally to agility anymore. She told me that Jane had been the dog's sole care-giver and had walked her every day no matter what the weather. She told me how proud she was of her daughter and that getting Sally had made them both genuinely happy, a welcome change from their terrible sadness brought on by the tragic loss of her husband. Sally had slept on Jane's bed since day one. Her mother described them as inseparable from the moment they met, through all those years.

"It was a match made in heaven," she told me, until just a few weeks ago, when out of the blue, Sally had growled at Jane for the very first time. Since then she had growled at her every time she had seen her. Her face clouded over and the smile of a moment ago vanished without trace. She concluded the explanation of their relationship with some haunting words and a wistful look: "Sally has been such a blessing to us both; I just don't know what Jane would have done without her." She was sad as she continued, "I don't know what *I* would have done without Sally, after my... well, after..." Her voice trailed off before finishing the sentence, and I watched her face as she relived the memory of losing her husband – Jane's father – so suddenly. My heart felt very heavy in sympathy with her sadness.

SALLY: THE MIRACLE OF DOGS

What could possibly have happened to change such a strong bond into a growling distance, I wondered? I asked her when the growling had started and what had been happening at the time.

"Jane came home from school and Sally met her at the door as she always did. I was in the hall, I saw the greeting and everything seemed normal: Sally was overjoyed to see Jane, as always." I noticed that as she continued to relive the memory, the lady ceased the stroking and withdrew her hand from Sally's head and placed it on her own lap, out of reach of the little dog. It's odd how a person can tell you what they are feeling by the unconscious acts of their body.

"As Jane bent down to hug her, Sally just suddenly pulled back and growled at her. Jane thought she had hurt her and went toward her again to hold her, to see what was wrong, but Sally backed off and showed her teeth. It was so sudden and horrid. Jane tried again to reach out to Sally, but Sally backed away even further and snarled and snarled at Jane. Ever since that moment, Sally has growled at Jane whenever she goes near her."

I watched as Sally stretched her neck long and nuzzled at the lady's hand, wanting the stroking to recommence. The mother's attention was brought back from the bad memory and into the moment by Sally's nudges and her hand returned to the little dog's head while the stroking recommenced, to Sally's seeming satisfaction. Pain. It had to be, surely? I had already heard that Sally had been diagnosed with arthritis and she had stopped doing agility. Perhaps she was having an arthritic flare-up? And Jane's hug had hurt her?

"Have you taken Sally back to the vet?" I enquired. "Sometimes this behaviour can be a sign of pain or worsening pain. Oftentimes dogs can carry huge amounts of pain before showing it. In fact sometimes sudden onsets of aggressive symptoms can be the only indication of pain in a dog. Is she currently on any medication?"

I was told that she had taken Sally to the vet and he had run all sorts of tests and done X-rays. But apart from the already diagnosed arthritis, there was nothing to suggest that Sally was in increased pain. The vet, very sensibly, had prescribed a week's worth of additional painkillers to see if it might improve the situation, but there had been no improvement at all. In fact, the behaviour had worsened. Now Sally wouldn't even sit in a room with Jane and had not slept on her bed, or even in her room, since the original growling incident.

Hmm. Not pain then, it seemed.

My questions continued but nothing stood out as a likely cause. Somewhat cautiously I asked if Jane was in and if she would be willing to speak with me herself.

The mother's face fell into despair and she looked at the floor for a few moments. Jane had been so upset by it all, she said, that she had hoped that I might be able to 'fix' Sally without having to involve Jane at all. Every time Jane and Sally were in the same room it all seemed to get even worse, she said. And she was not sure that Jane could take much more upset. Since the first day of growling, Jane had taken to spending more and more time in her bedroom, alone. She was getting depressed again. The mother had heard her crying often. She had gone to the daughter when she heard her tears, but it seemed Jane's sadness could not be alleviated by her mother's love, only by her dog. The dog who did not want to be near her.

She had cried and cried for days, she told me, and now at night Jane was having cold sweats and nightmares too and at times had cried out in her sleep, calling Sally's name.

She looked directly at me as she continued, "I am going to have to take her to the doctor soon to see what can be done.

She has been so upset and now she won't even talk to me about it. Her whole world has fallen apart without Sally…" She paused for a moment, as she remembered "And it reminds me of when…" Her face crumpled slightly, her bottom lip quivered with emotion. Her voice trailed off and tears filled her eyes. She was, I suspected, once again remembering the tragic death of her husband.

It was a heart-wrenching tale and my own heart screamed out in pain for each of them. How awful. I felt the burden of responsibility bearing down on me – I needed to resolve this situation and I needed to resolve it fast. But how?

"Oh my goodness, I am so very sorry." I reached out a hand to her. She smiled weakly at me, acknowledged my act, but brushed it aside and instead reached for a tissue to wipe her eyes and nose.

I looked at Sally to see if she could provide any insight; she flipped her tail at me but continued to seek affection from her owner. She just didn't look like the growling sort.

I had no wish to upset the lady's daughter further but I needed to see Sally's reaction to her for myself, and I needed to speak with Jane to see if she could offer any more clues, because at that moment I really didn't know where to go with this case and I soooo wanted to help. But I had no idea at this stage what could transform what sounded like a very strong bond between a dog and its loving owner into tatters.

After some thought the lady agreed she would go upstairs and ask Jane if she might come down and speak with me. She left the room. As she began to ascend the stairs I heard her footfall, heavy and slow. I noted that as I heard it, Sally started to become agitated. The little dog got up from where she was and came over to me and once again she tried to climb onto my lap. This time, she was quite forceful and I had to push hard to keep her off. I wanted to see how she coped when Jane arrived, without being supported by me. Sally looked wary and worried.

A few minutes passed during which I heard muffled talking from the upstairs room. Then I heard the bedroom door open, followed by a set of footsteps on the creaky stairs, soon to be followed by a second set of footsteps, those of Jane I presumed.

On hearing this, Sally left my side and moved further away to the far side of the room. She knew, it seemed, that Jane was coming and she wanted to get as far away as possible from the door that Jane would come through. She began to pant and lick her lips and look around for a way out.

The door opened and the mother walked in, soon followed by the sad, tired-looking, tear-stained daughter. She was wearing pyjamas and a dressing gown – it looked like she had been in bed this afternoon. They entered the room quietly. Sally grew more agitated. She glanced at Jane warily from the far side of the room and I heard a low, deep growl. Jane sat next to her mother on the sofa, at the furthest point from Sally. Sally began to pace up and down by the radiator like a caged animal, looking for a way to escape. She kept glancing at Jane, freezing for a moment, uttering a growl and then pacing again. Her hackles were risen in arousal and her panting intensified as she licked saliva from her lips.

Jane sat immobile, just staring at the floor as I observed her. Her mother placed a protective arm around the sad girl to comfort her. This was so hard for all three of them. Momentarily, I saw Jane glance briefly at Sally. As Jane witnessed Sally's discomfort under her stare, she looked back at the floor as her eyes filled with tears. Jane knew that she was the source of her much-loved dog's fear. Her mother saw her tears, passed her a tissue, and tried to pull her closer, but Jane resisted and sat immobile, and stiff, as if frozen.

She took the tissue but just clutched it, as though it had no purpose.

I had never sensed such deep sadness in any person and as I looked at them both, I realised that this case above any other I had ever seen was one entrenched in despair and deep-rooted pain.

It was time for me to speak, so I did. "Thank you for coming to see me, Jane. I'm so sorry that you are having such an upsetting time with Sally. She seems such a sweet girl and it must be so horrid for you to see her this way." I stumbled for more words. I hadn't planned what I was going to say and suddenly I felt myself made wordless by the apparent hopelessness of the situation.

The mother looked at me, willing me to say something more, pain and pleading etched upon her face. She wanted me to provide some hope, to give them an answer, a solution. But I was simply dumbstruck for a moment with the sadness that enveloped us all.

Looking at the distress in Sally, Jane and her mother I decided to call a halt to the suffering, at least for the little dog. "Thank you Jane for coming down to see me, I can see how sad you are and I will help all that I can." Then I made a promise I was not sure that I could keep, but I needed to give them both hope. "I promise I will keep working with you until we resolve this. Feel free to go back upstairs if you wish." I just hoped that in a moment something would just 'come to me', as it sometimes did.

As she stood up slowly, Jane again glanced once more at Sally, who was now pinned in the corner, panting heavily. She tried and failed to stem another sob as she saw the fear in her much-loved dog's eyes. Her mother stood with her and as Jane turned to leave, an arm was once again placed around her daughter and gently, she escorted the sobbing girl from the room and away from the worried dog, back upstairs. "Come on," she said, "let's get you tucked up in bed." And Jane was gone. I was alone once more with my confused thoughts and Sally, the cause of all the confusion.

As the door closed behind them, Sally seemed to heave a sigh of relief and her attitude and behaviour began to calm. She came to me and sat at my side once more, seeking comfort.

What on earth could have caused this terrible, heart-breaking situation? I just stared at and stroked Sally, needing comfort myself. I felt like all the life and energy had been drained from me. I had no idea what was wrong; no idea what to do. I just sat there feeling useless and drained.

I reached once more for my mug of tea, hoping there might still be a swallow of fluid left and within it, perhaps some inspiration. As I lifted the cup I saw just a stain at the bottom where the much-cherished drink had been, but a memory suddenly flashed through my mind.

"Do you want a cup of tea?" I heard again the words that he had spoken. A memory of an old, wise shepherd who I had met once many years ago at a sheepdog trial. He had taken pity on me as I was so frozen with cold and had offered me some tea from his flask, which I gratefully received. His hair was almost white with age and his skin told the tale of many decades of weather. We had got to chatting about his life in the mountains with no one but dogs as companions, the magic of sheepdogs and how wonderful dogs are in general. There are few things that I enjoy more than listening to wise dog folk, so I was a sponge for his every word, as he regaled me with many wonderful tales while we sat together for several hours. Later in the day he told me a story that I found utterly fascinating, if rather hard to believe. That one of his dogs, his favourite one at the time, had once saved his life by 'telling' him that he was ill. How for weeks his dog had persistently behaved oddly toward him and had pestered him, pushing his nose into the man's stomach; an act that the wise 'dog-man' had not understood.

The dog's persistence had bothered the shepherd. He had never seen a dog behave this way and he suspected that the dog was trying to tell him something important. Increasingly perplexed by the dog's continuous harassment, the man had eventually gone to see a doctor; he needed to tell someone of his concerns about his dog's behaviour and the fact that it bugged him so much. He had thought perhaps that the doctor might conclude that he was going mad, receiving messages from dogs. The old country-wise doctor had listened and then checked the man over. Later tests revealed that the dog had in fact been indicating a tumour that was beginning to develop inside the shepherd.

The old man believed that without the dog's 'early warning system' he would have died; the doctor had confirmed this. He had buried his favourite dog in the flowerbed of bluebells after the dog had lived out his retirement lying by the fire. Every day he went to that spot in the garden and thanked the dog for giving him back his life. "Always be grateful for what you have and live every day as if it might be your last," he had advised me, and then he concluded with the important words: "And always trust your favourite dog."

Those wise words had stayed with me. Could it be that Sally had detected something wrong with Jane? Was the dog reacting so badly, not to Jane as such, but to something *within* Jane? I didn't know why, but it just felt to me as if it might be the case. Why else would this memory have come to me right at this time? Sometimes no matter where you search or what questions you ask, only intuition can tell you the true story. Was the memory of the shepherd trying to speak to me as his dog had spoken to him? If it wasn't this, then I didn't know what else it could be.

The door opened and the mother returned and sat down. She looked older than she had even a few minutes ago. The strain of her daughter's sadness was eating away at her energy. "So what do you think is wrong with Sally?" She looked up at me expectantly.

I thought for several more seconds before replying, as I was still so uncertain and didn't know how I could get her to take me seriously. I tried to deliver the news carefully, knowing I could still be wrong. I hoped I was wrong – I didn't want for Jane to be ill. But if it was not this, then what was it?

In times of uncertainty when dealing with owners and their dogs, I have a rule that I follow. Delivering bad news is not easy, especially if you don't know if the bad news is actually true or not. Whenever I find it hard to explain, I follow a simple rule that means that I have done the best I can: Be kind and be honest.

"I realise that this is probably a weird thing to hear, but I am beginning to wonder if Sally has seen some illness in Jane that is making her behave this way. Some animals seem to know these things. I am wondering if there is something wrong with Jane, and Sally is trying to tell us? Something Sally can smell or sense somehow?" The uncertainty in my voice must have been evident to the mother as her face started to contort into one of disbelief. So I tried to back up my statement. "I have heard of other cases where this has happened." Her previously open enquiring face showed doubt and anger. She realised that I was talking of something I had no direct personal experience of, only something I had heard of. I expect the pressure of the previous few weeks had made her short-tempered.

She looked at me, utterly aghast. "Are you suggesting that the dog is a doctor? Have you been in this job very long? Perhaps you need a change of career!" She sounded angry and sarcastic. "Don't be so absurd!" she said, as she waved her hand at me in a dismissive fashion before continuing, "Is that *really* all you can come up with?" She sighed heavily and turned her head away from me in disgust for a few moments, as she apparently studied the wall opposite.

Seemingly having made up her mind, she turned back to face me and as she did, she stood up. All the sadness had left her face and had been replaced by pure anger. She pointed to me and then to the door. "I'd like you to leave now, please!"

Oh no! What had I done? I had come here to help, but now I had made everything worse. I opened my mouth to try to explain some more but she just wanted me gone.

Her voice had risen now. "GET OUT!"

I had failed them. I left the house with my head bowed and my heart aching.

★

For the next two years or so I pondered the case, but spoke to no one of it. I felt I had completely failed them and loused the whole thing up. I didn't want to publicise my failure so I kept the events in my own heart where I went over and over them, berating and doubting myself and telling myself how hopeless I was. I felt foolish and ashamed. I didn't know for sure if Sally had detected something in Jane or not, but I did know that if that was not the case, then I had failed to diagnose the real problem, or come up with any solution to help them. I hoped with all my heart that they had managed to find someone else who could understand Sally's behaviour. Someone better than me.

Maybe I wasn't so good at this job after all.

And then, around two years after the visit, I was standing with my shopping trolley in a long queue at the supermarket. I first felt and then saw someone looking at me from the next serving point. She too was standing in a long queue. I thought I recognised her face but couldn't quite place it. She looked as if she recognised me and spoke cautiously. "Denise McLeod?" she enquired.

"Yes," I answered, still trying to place her.

She came closer to me. "Do you remember Sally, the dog who growled at my daughter?"

Bang! The memory hit me like a gunshot and I flushed with the embarrassment of the failure of that day and the shame I had felt ever since.

"You were right about Sally! Jane was diagnosed with cancer soon after we saw you. She had treatment right away and has recently been given the all-clear!" She beamed a smile I had never seen before. But her face changed again as she continued, "I am so sorry for what I said to you and how I treated you. That I doubted you as I did. I should have rung you to tell you afterwards, but I felt so embarrassed at my own behaviour." She paused and looked at the floor. "I just wasn't thinking straight at the time with so much upset going on, and your suggestion just sounded so, well, ridiculous."

Whoosh! Two years' worth of guilt and shame washed right off me and away into the ether. Just like that, it was gone.

She continued, "What you said seemed so silly, but I couldn't shake it off and no one else I saw could suggest anything else that could be wrong with Sally. So I did take Jane to the doctor. He didn't believe me when I told him what you had said, but he ran some tests anyway. Then he was able to diagnose cancer, and treatment commenced. The doctor said that had it not been for Sally's early warning, the outcome might have been very different." Emotion caught her before she concluded: "Thank you, so much – you may well have saved my daughter's life!"

I was overjoyed at this news. I looked upwards to where the sky would have been had we not been in a shop, and silently I thanked that shepherd from all those years ago, and his dog that he had buried under the bluebells. I had no idea if the old man might still be alive, but it felt right to look skyward as I thanked them both for saving Jane.

I was busting with happiness but then I remembered little Sally, pinned against the radiator in fear, and asked how things were now.

Sally was fine. "She and Jane are best friends again now and everything has gone back to normal." She told me that Sally's arthritic legs were getting worse but Jane had started to take her to hydrotherapy and had decided that she wanted to be a vet, to help dogs like Sally, just as Sally had helped her.

She beamed at me again. "Aren't dogs magical!"

They certainly are.

★

The relationship between dogs and humans goes back many thousands of years. Some suggestions say 40,000; some say more, some say less. But what is for sure is that for a very long time dogs have been observing, watching over, and caring for humans in the same way that humans have been watching over and caring for dogs. It is perhaps no surprise then that animals, as closely linked with humans as dogs are, have developed these abilities to detect abnormalities and take action to bring them to our attention.

Since Sally's case, I have met or talked with a number of people who have reported that their pet dog has alerted them to potential health problems, from seizures and fits to low blood sugar levels in diabetics, through to those that detect cancer. It is really quite common. However it is not common, from what

I now understand, for a dog to react in the same way as Sally did, with growling or aggressive signals. I suspect that Sally was growling not *at* Jane but at what was *in Jane,* that she did not like. Far more common is a dog that barks, nudges or paws at an owner, or the care-giver of a sick child, or one which licks or nuzzles the affected area like the old shepherd's dog did. So if your dog behaves oddly at around the same time that you or one of your relatives is sick or feels about to be sick, or you can trace a change of behaviour back to a time when a relative might have developed a cancer or other medical problem, then consider that the dog may not be being disruptive or naughty (though he might be), but instead that he might be fulfilling a very valuable and potentially life-saving assistance process.

Apparently, many dogs learn this skill just by spending time in the presence of their family and observing what happens when a medical situation does arise. But now there are charities and companies that actually train dogs to detect cancer cells or alert to seizures or other illnesses, both at home and in laboratory conditions, where a person's samples are sent for analysis 'by dog'.

Whilst it is thought that most of these dogs are detecting bodily changes using their extraordinary sense of smell, which is millions of times more effective than a human's, I have also heard of more than one dog who can alert that an issue is arising when they are not even near the human in question, ruling out the possibility of the dog using just its nose to detect a problem. One of my own friend's dogs, the lovely Ace, taught himself to alert in advance to her daughter's seizure events. One day, the dog began to alert even though the child was over five miles away, staying with a grandparent. *Now just HOW did he do that?* What's more, that same dog, as he aged, began to teach her younger dog how to do the same, meaning that when so sadly Ace died of old age recently, her other dog, Buddy, took over the role of alert dog. How amazing is that!

In the UK, the charity Medical Detection Dogs trains dogs to sniff samples of urine, faeces, or breath, or skin swabs. The dogs work on samples in the bio-detection room at the training centre and are not trained to detect the odour on a person.

But there are other charities, businesses and organisations that train dogs to detect seizures, diabetic episodes or other medical issues in the owner's home, and still more that offer training to pet owners who wish for their dogs to alert to a family member.

So if you or a family member has medical concerns, then why not check out if your dog can be trained to help alert to the onset of an episode of illness?

Or if your own dog behaves oddly at times, then please consider that he might be trying to tell you something important. He might be fully aware that a seizure is about to occur, or your blood sugar levels may be failing, or something sinister may be growing inside you. Remember; always trust your favourite dog. Aren't dogs amazing!

★

So much time has passed since the case of Sally that she must now have crossed the rainbow bridge, so to Sally I thank you for teaching me and for saving Jane and for giving rise to this knowledge that I now have. And to gorgeous Ace, thank you for helping as you did and for being an inspiration to so many with your special talents. You were a gorgeous, lovely, kind boy who performed real animal magic in your self-adopted role as alert dog. Run free, handsome boy.

Simba: The Perfect Dog

One of the things that fascinates me, and was unexpected when I began working in dog training and behaviour, is the huge variety of people, life events, complex relationships, diversity of points of view and surprises that I encounter as part of my daily work, not just with dogs, but with dog owners. Each day brings with it different challenges and surprises – some good, some bad; some enlightening, others mysterious and dark. Today it was the turn of mystery to challenge me.

"Hello, is that the dog lady?" It was a friendly, gentle voice, but weary and somewhat cautious.

"Yes, hello. How can I help?"

"I've got some problems with my dog and I wondered if you could come to see him, please?"

"Okay, what problems are you having?" I wanted to establish the facts of the case.

"*Tell her about the car.*" A man's voice in the background. Perhaps I was on speaker phone?

There was a pause and then: "Oh, lots of problems, he doesn't like the car, for one."

"Oh, in what way does he not like the car?" I needed to know more.

"He just doesn't like it," came the immediate reply.

18

"What makes you say that? What does he do in the car that concerns you?" I didn't understand her reluctance to share details.

"He just doesn't like it."

"But what exactly does he *do* in the car?"

Without me discovering what made them think he didn't like the car, the conversation suddenly changed direction with another intervention from the man's voice, slightly louder than before but still in the background: "Tell her how bad he is on walks." Three-way conversations are never easy.

Failing to answer my questions about the car, she spoke again. "Well that's not the only problem."

"Oh? What else is the matter?"

"He's not very good on walks."

I continued to dig for information. Getting to the root of the problem under discussion can sometimes be a lengthy and challenging process. She seemed reluctant, unsure as to what exactly was wrong with her own dog.

"Oh dear. What does he do on walks that makes you say that?"

"He just misbehaves." Another spurious answer.

"In what way?" I could see this being a very long day indeed!

"Well, he won't do what he is told."

I made my questions more direct.

"What do you ask him to do that he doesn't do?"

"Anything and everything!" Again, she sounded like she didn't believe her own words somehow, almost as if she was just making it up!

"Give me an example!" I was getting frustrated.

She too sounded somewhat exasperated. It was not an easy conversation for either of us. "He's just not very good. Can you please come round and see him?"

It seemed that she simply wasn't able to tell me what was wrong. So I changed tack, and quizzed her on problems that were common in dogs. I tried to guess the problem, hoping for yes or no answers that might clarify things. I asked about the most common problem that I encounter. "How is he with other dogs when out on walks?"

Her voice changed and lightened up, she sounded pleased as she answered, "Oh, he's fine with dogs. No problem with other dogs at all."

"Does he pull on the lead?" I delved.

Again, she sounded pleased; proud even. "Oh no, not really, He's never really been a puller."

"Is he okay with people?"

The conversation was starting to flow more easily as she began to tell me how good her dog was. "Oh yes, he likes people. He is well-mannered and polite with them, but friendly."

He sounded like a great dog to me. "Okay, does he come to you when you call him?" She was starting to sound really happy as she reeled off all the things that were not wrong with her dog! I was beginning to wonder if I would ever actually find out what *was* wrong.

"Oh yes, sometimes I have to yell at him, if there are rabbits about, but mostly he is okay at coming back to me."

He was friendly with people and dogs, his recall was acceptable. He already sounds better than most dogs I met out walking, so what could be wrong? I changed tack again.

"Have you walked him today?"

"Yes I have. This morning." She still sounded positive.

"Tell me about that walk. What happened today?" I was beginning to feel like a psychiatrist with a reluctant client, asking all these questions, getting very few answers. My mind flitted briefly and in it I saw her lying on a couch in front of me as I continued to quiz her.

"Oh, just the usual." She started to clam up again. It dawned on me that she might be lying. But why? Why ring for my help only to lie to me? I felt I was on a merry-go-round that I might never get off.

"The usual?"

"Yes, nothing new, just like he always is." I sensed real exasperation in her voice now as she continued, "I just want you to come and see the dog, I would like you to come for three hours, please."

I don't do consults for three hours. Three hours is too long for me and often too long for dog and owner, as I explained. But she was adamant that she wanted me for three hours. I tried and failed with further questioning but in the end I just gave in and agreed to go see this dog who seemingly had no problems. Maybe the dog would find it easier to explain his own problems when I saw him? I was suspicious. I liked her voice, but there seemed to be something not quite right here. She had been lying, of that I grew increasingly sure.

★

Before leaving later that week for the consult at their home, I did as I usually do and told a friend of the location of my appointment and what time I was due to arrive and leave. When visiting a stranger's home, it's always good to make sure someone knows where you are, especially when you are going to see a 'problem dog' who apparently has no problems and an owner who sounds like she isn't telling you the truth.

When I arrived at their large, detached house, in an affluent area, I drove up via a long, sweeping gravel driveway. I parked the car and walked somewhat cautiously to the door. By the door was a bench placed in the afternoon sun. It had a hand-carved summer scene etched into the backrest. It looked so welcoming, I wanted to sit on it to enjoy the sunshine and go no further. I already felt weary and had not been looking forward to this appointment at all. But instead, I tentatively knocked the door. I was nervous.

The face I encountered as she opened the door was friendly but tired looking. Her husband stayed back from the door and didn't speak to me, instead I saw him scuttling off into a room at the back of the house and he closed the door. It made me feel uncomfortable. Over her shoulder I could see up the long corridor toward the back of the house. I noticed a number of very beautiful antiques; odd furniture for such a new house. Then the dog appeared and he walked slowly and calmly towards me with a gently wagging tail. He greeted me with quiet, well-mannered respect, with all four paws on the floor, and again I wondered what could be 'wrong' with him.

As she got her dog's lead and put on her shoes, she started to chat in a friendly fashion and advised me that we were going to the woods in the car to walk the dog.

I really wasn't sure that I wanted to go to the woods with this woman and her apparently faultless dog. I still didn't know *why* I was there. So before committing to going to the woods with this stranger, I again tried to establish what was wrong with the dog.

"So far, I really don't understand why you want help with your dog. To me he seems a really nice fella. Please tell me, if I had a magic wand and could change one thing about your dog, what would it be?"

The 'magic wand' question usually helped people understand their own desires. The concept seemed to open their minds to all possibilities and free them to discuss things in a more open way. It was often the trump card that paved the way to success in understanding an owner's desires for their dog.

She paused and looked at me for a moment, and I sensed she understood my frustration and confusion. She quietly closed the door behind her so that her husband couldn't hear what she was about to divulge. Then she leaned towards me conspiratorially, and beckoned me to draw closer. Some truth was about to come forth.

"There's nothing wrong with the dog." Aha! The truth at last. "My husband hates the dog. He blames the dog for everything that is wrong in our lives."

Poor dog. As she spoke, the words flowed, the blockage had been lifted and now she spoke the truth, her face lightened and she became open and warm. She loved her dog – that was clear. She was proud of him. He was a good dog; I could already see that as he stood patiently at her side, on a loose lead, awaiting her next move.

"I'll tell you more when we get to the woods. Come on, let's get going!"

I liked her now she had told me the truth, so feeling more confident I got into my car and she into hers. We set off to the woods for a long walk and an even longer conversation. As we walked, her dog, Simba, romped around happily. I observed his responsiveness to her. He had good manners, approached others calmly and with respect, and I could see nothing for me to help with.

But she sure wanted to talk! She told me of their recent move to the area. After a number of family traumas, traumas which had nearly ended their marriage, they had moved to this, a new area, to escape the bad memories and hoped that in so doing, their marriage might improve. She felt lonely and isolated here, so far from her friends at her old house. They had quarrelled increasingly but she was adamant that she must fix this marriage as she knew she could never survive alone, she said. My heart went out to her.

We walked and talked and she seemed to gain relief from unburdening herself.

"My husband is always blaming the dog and it was he that insisted that I call you. To sort the dog out, he said. But there is nothing wrong with Simba. The problem is my husband! Maybe you could help me with him?" She laughed as she said it. It's a surprisingly common question and one which people ask with some mirth, but one which I had learned sometimes had a serious undercurrent: "Do you solve problems with my husband/wife/mother-in-law?!"

After she had unburdened herself it was time to leave and we returned to the cars to bid farewell. And there she dropped the bombshell I had dreaded: "Would you mind coming back with me and explaining to my husband that there is nothing wrong with Simba? He is always so mean and Simba doesn't deserve it. Will you help Simba by doing this?" Her eyes pleaded with me. She had played the guilt card, a card that I suspected was frequently thrown down in her marital relationship. My heart sank. She wanted me to help the dog, by helping her to prove her husband wrong. It's not a role I was comfortable with but I did want to help Simba if I could. He was such a lovely, gentle soul. I wasn't sure I'd ever met a more well-mannered animal. It seemed so sad that her husband could not see it.

"It was my husband who insisted I call you," she told me again, "and it was he who said I needed to see you for three hours, even though I knew that there was nothing wrong with Simba. Anything for an easy life, so I gave in and agreed. At least he said he would pay for it!" She smiled darkly as she said it. The thought of pointlessly depriving her own husband of money seemed to at least bring her some satisfaction.

Sadly, when I work with couples or visit people's homes, I see many relationships in trouble. So many family tragedies, so many broken hearts, failed relationships, upset, anger and disillusionment in the people who share their lives with the dogs I work with. Conversely, I sometimes, very luckily, encounter outstanding, supportive relationships that bring joy to one's soul. People who thrive on honesty, sharing, giving, gratitude and a real wonder at the miracle of life. These people bring peace and pleasure to me and often to their dogs too. But today sadly it was the former, not the latter that I must face. So, reluctantly, I agreed.

As we waited for the traffic to clear so that we could cross the carriageway and turn into her driveway, I was anxious. I didn't want to speak to the husband, but I did want to help Simba. I thought briefly of switching off my indicator and just driving off, never to be seen again.

The road cleared and her car pulled smartly away in front of me and passed through the gateway onto her gravelled drive. I was but a few feet behind her. As we started to gain speed on the drive I engaged second gear when suddenly and abruptly, her car stopped dead in front of me. I saw Simba, in the boot of the car, lurch forward. I slammed my foot on the brake and narrowly avoided hitting her car. The gravel crunched beneath my wheels. I waited to see what would happen next. Had she run out of petrol? Stalled the car? I waited. Nothing happened. I could see her just sitting there, unmoving. After a few minutes, I got out of my car to see if she was okay. I approached her car with trepidation. She was clutching the steering wheel and staring, fixedly, straight ahead. She didn't notice me. I looked to see what she was staring at. I couldn't see anything out of the ordinary.

Then she moved and slowly opened the door, and ignoring me completely as if lost in her own world, started to walk tentatively towards her house, keys in her hand. I followed behind and as we walked I asked, "Are you okay, what's wrong?" There was no reply. She walked cautiously, stiffly ahead.

Curious and concerned, I followed behind like a lost puppy, not knowing what was happening. As we got to the front door I noticed that the beautiful carved wooden bench I'd so admired earlier was gone. The imprint of its former position was still evident in the gravel. Had she been burgled? I stood with her as she unlocked the door and stepped into her hall. The silence between us was deafening. I followed on behind, still baffled as to what was happening. As we entered the hallway I noticed that the lovely antiques that had been there previously were also missing. She must have been burgled. Oh no! My heart sank for her.

Once inside, she seemed suddenly invigorated and as I waited uncertainly in the large entrance hall, she paced into the kitchen at the back. Returning quickly, she went into the room at the side, reappearing moments later. Nearly running now, she passed me in the hall and ascended the stairs two at a time. Her face was fixed in shock, her cheeks glowing red. I waited below, not knowing what to do. I saw her enter a room, and then finally she spoke.

"The bastard!" She spat out the words in anger. "He's taken everything and moved out!"

Her husband's complaints about the dog and the three-hour consult were just a ruse to get her out of the house and have adequate time to take the most valuable items of furniture and all of his important personal effects, and he had left her. How awful for her.

She sat down on the bottom step of the stairs, put her head in her hands and cried. And here I was. I'd come to help with her dog, but now found myself in the centre of an emotional minefield. I did the only thing I could do and suggested that I make a cup of tea. Thankfully he had not taken the kettle and as I waited for it to boil I could hear her sobbing back in the hall. I took tea to her and then went outside to retrieve Simba, who was still sitting waiting patiently in the car. Once back inside we sat on the stairs, as all the furniture had gone, and we drank tea together. There in that moment of sadness she somehow decided that I was her only friend in the world and later when she had calmed and I tried to leave, she clung to me, thanking me and begging me, a virtual stranger, to help her through this. A surprising and tragic twist to a very weird day, but I agreed to help however I could. What else could I do?

★

For the next three weeks I became the centre of her world. She would call me in the night, sobbing. She begged me to walk with her each day and although I had other things that I needed to do, I agreed. I felt so sorry for her. As we walked she updated me daily on progress. She had not heard from her husband and had no idea where he had gone. She couldn't afford to live in the house alone. What should she do? Some days she seemed brighter and almost relieved that he had gone; other days she cried and told me she couldn't go on without him. And so it proceeded, day after day. Simba and my dogs developed a good relationship as we walked each day together and I began to really fall in love with him. He was so gentle, balanced and well-mannered. He was lovely. He was also very supportive towards her. He sat at her side and licked her hand. The relationship between them was strong and for that I was most grateful. She had Simba and Simba had her. That, at least, was a blessing.

Then one day, I went to her house to walk with her as usual and she wasn't there. I called her on my mobile phone. The house phone rang out, then went to answering machine and I left a message before driving home. I tried to call many times, and returned to the house again to see what had befallen her, but I never heard from her, or saw her again. Soon, a 'For Sale' board appeared outside her home and I was left wondering what on earth had happened to her and Simba. I missed them. We had all become friends and my dogs and hers had enjoyed playing together.

The dog world is a small world, and a few months later a woman I'd never met before walked into an equestrian centre where I was about to start a new beginner's agility training course, holding the loose lead of a dog I recognised at once. Simba! Though he still had a relaxed, gentle manner, his soft eyes now bored into me. He wagged his tail vigorously when he saw me and pulled the owner right to me, so pleased was he to see me again.

I greeted the dog I'd spent so much time with and was pleased to see him looking so well. "Is this Simba?" I enquired. But I knew it was.

The lady smiled. "Yes, isn't he lovely! I've not had him long. I got him a few weeks back from a lady who said she had become allergic to him." She paused. "I didn't like the woman, I don't think she was telling me the truth. But I don't mind. Simba is such a good boy and he has slotted into our family life really well. He's great with my kids!" She beamed at him and then back at me. "I thought he might like to learn agility! He's a really clever dog and ever so well behaved."

This much I knew to be true. So Simba had a new and committed home. His former owners had both disappeared, the house was soon occupied by someone else and I was left wondering what on earth had happened to the lady I had spent three weeks of my life so deeply embroiled with. But

I never got to find out. I never heard from her again. What had started as a mysterious case ended as an even more mysterious case. But at least the dog I'd gone to see seemed happy and well-loved and so pleasingly for me, he was back in my life.

All's well that ends well!

Luna:
Don't Leave Me!

During my time working in dog training and behaviour I have met thousands and thousands of dogs, and with those thousands of dogs come even more thousands of people. It is simply impossible for me to remember all of those thousands of dogs and people, so when I look back at cases and clients, I mostly only remember those that were unusually 'good', or those that were unusually 'bad'. Or I remember the ones that taught me something, like those that I write about in this book.

In this case, I remember the family because they were exceptional in their utter commitment to their dog but also because they taught me something. In fact several things; not just about dogs, but about people too.

Luna was one of the first 'official' Labradoodle puppies that came into our classes. At the time the dog world was just accepting the change that was happening, when what most of us had called crossbreeds or mongrels or mutts suddenly became named 'breeds', like the Labradoodle. As I understand it, Labradoodles were originally bred in an effort to create an allergy-free alternative to Labradors for work as guide dogs for the blind. A worthwhile and valid cause, I thought. Since then, the breed has grown in popularity and numbers and the beginning of a new dawn of named crossbreeds had begun.

I studied all of the new breeds with interest, keen to know if they did indeed provide an allergy-free alternative, and with later crossbreeds, how they varied from the breeds from which they had been created; whether they developed their own breed standard in terms of character and behaviour. Interesting times.

Luna's owners arrived at the first night of the course, a dog-free introduction night that all our puppy owners are required to attend. They were first-time dog owners and alive with questions for me. It quickly became apparent that they had researched the 'breed' well and had read books and articles, bought magazines and visited numerous dog-training centres before choosing ours to attend with their very first puppy. They were clearly approaching this as a lifetime commitment and had every intention of getting it 'right', as best as they possibly could. The starting point for that evening's talk was, as always, a question to the audience: "Who has bought a dog, with the specific intention of doing with that dog what it has been bred to do?"

I asked the audience to raise their hands if they had. As usual, there were very few hands raised – an informative fact in itself.

But Luna's owners did raise their hands, so I asked them what it was they intended to do with their Labradoodle. "We want a Labrador-type dog, but my husband is severely allergic to dogs, so we bought this breed, which apparently will not produce an allergic reaction," came the reply. Fair enough.

As the fun-filled event went on, it was clear that this family, polite and interested, friendly and engaging, wanted to drag out every ounce of my knowledge as they fired questions at me, so that they could best understand the task ahead of them, that of turning a well-adjusted puppy into a well-adjusted dog. I loved their level of enthusiasm and the quality of their questions. This was a family whose dog I would enjoy seeing develop, I was sure. I couldn't wait to meet the subject of such effort, and watch as she grew and matured.

*

The following week the family arrived, accompanied by Luna, then eleven weeks old. Luna was quite a sensitive and shy puppy and it took a few minutes for her to come out from under the chair, but it wasn't long before her confidence grew and she became relaxed and happy in the class.

The family sucked up every bit of teaching I gave like bread dipped in gravy and they were diligent in their practice at home. They asked astute and sensible questions and listened attentively as I answered. Despite their lack of experience, they were soon streaking ahead of the class in terms of results through their sheer commitment and dedication to the dog.

The children were polite and well-mannered and sat quietly as their parents took turns to train some of the exercises with Luna. Then at other times, they took their own turn to do an exercise. Everything was going really well and their positivity and commitment was invigorating to be around.

I grew to admire their commitment, but also their love and respect for one another. The whole family seemed to thrive together and Luna, though always a quiet, reflective animal, appeared to have even more appreciation and fondness for them than I did. No one else in the room mattered to her except her family.

It's funny how having one really attentive and hard-working set of owners in a group can lift the spirits of the instructor, as well as the rest of the group. The fact that they worked so hard on exercises at home and therefore advanced so well and so fast motivated the rest of the class to do the same, and the whole group became a joy to teach and spend time with. It was one of my favourite groups of dogs out of the thousands that I have taught. Even after many years have passed, that group still sticks in my mind, because of that one family and the effect they had on the others.

Sadly though, it wasn't long before a problem developed. My respect for the likeable and committed family began to grow even greater. She rang me to say that it seemed her husband was allergic to this dog after all, and was there anything she could do to minimise the allergy-producing variable in the dog whilst at classes? Was there anything at all that I could do or suggest to help the situation? I had no idea how to help with allergies at home so I apologised and said sorry, no. All I could think of for the times spent at class was for him to stand outside the room and look through the window, to watch them training, so that he avoided contact with Luna and the other dogs.

I had begun to notice that the husband had been sitting slightly away from Luna in class, and that he had stopped handling her, though she focused on him more than anyone else. The man had started to show signs of being really poorly in class, and then one day, for the first time, he wasn't there. I asked after him and was told he had arranged a few days away on business so that he could have some recovery time away from Luna and the allergy that she created in him. The lady told me that they had never spent nights apart all the time they had been married and they all missed him dearly. But he needed time away to recover from the reaction Luna created in him, even though it seemed it was still getting worse.

A pattern emerged. One week he came and sniffed and wheezed his way through class and then he would be missing for a week. The dog still continued to progress and the whole group stayed together. For course after course they kept returning and they were way beyond the normal level of training for adolescent dogs. Luna was still top of the class, although the husband came less and less often. One day his wife came to speak to me and was beaming.

"We have found a solution to Graham's allergy, we think." She smiled at me. It turned out that they had decided to invest a good deal of money into extending the house, building a large room at the front. The room was sealed off from the rest of the house, had a shower in it and a wardrobe to house all of Graham's freshly laundered clothes. Whenever he left home for work, he would go into a small sealed room, take off his clothes and put them in to a laundry basket. He then stepped into another sealed room to shower, then he exited the shower in the opposite direction into the new room, which contained only clean clothes which had been laundered externally by a third party. They kept all the husband's clothes separate from the family's clothes. Having showered and dressed in the isolation room he would now be free of the causative allergic effects of Luna, whilst he 'recovered' at work. He had even changed his job to one that demanded he spent great chunks of time working away. They missed each other but he simply couldn't cope with the illness without the increasingly long breaks to recover. I was stunned at this unique and brilliant idea, and wished them great luck.

Although the shower room and clothes isolation process did help, the man's condition improved only slightly and temporarily, and he soon discovered that he needed to spend more and more time away from home, to recover.

At no point, though, did they *ever* consider rehoming the dog. And although the wife jokingly remarked that she had considered rehoming the husband, I knew she wasn't serious.

One day we chatted about how the husband, who was absent from class that week, was doing and she smiled and said cheerily, "Well we will only have Luna for ten to fifteen years, so it's only a temporary thing, him being away." A temporary thing! To me, living apart from my husband for ten to fifteen years would have been a massive thing. To them, it was just a passing inconvenience that allowed them to keep their dog and 'get by for now' with their marriage. If it had been possible, my respect for them would have grown further. Again I was incredulous at the commitment of this entire family to their dog and felt so sad that Luna had not provided the allergy-free solution they had hoped for.

Eventually he stopped coming to classes, as his illness prevented it, and finally she rang to say that sadly and reluctantly they had decided they could no longer come as they felt that after dog-training nights her husband grew worse, whether he had attended or not. The wife and children, it seemed, were infecting him after every class they came to. I was genuinely saddened, but I totally understood. My heart went out to them all and I wished them the very best of luck. I would miss them all and I told them so. And so Luna and her delightful family left my life.

★

Many weeks later, I received a phone call from the lady owner. Luna, she said, had begun to suffer from 'separation anxiety' – not at home, but when the family left her outside a shop.

Separation anxiety is one of the most common problems that dogs and owners have to deal with and this case helped me to start thinking about it in new ways.

She gave me some background to the case in hand. The husband's allergies had worsened since we had last spoken and he was now routinely living away from home during the week, returning only at weekends. Even when at home, sadly, he had to stay away from Luna as much as possible and he only really spent time with her when they were outdoors walking. Wherever possible he walked 'up wind' of Luna to minimise the risk of allergy. As a result of this, they were walking more and more, so the family could all spend time with their dog and the children with their dad. As it was summer, they had taken to walking a long route that involved a stop at an ice cream shop at the halfway mark, where the whole family, including Luna, enjoyed an ice cream.

"We need the ice cream for the calories we burn up walking all day," she giggled. What an amazingly positive attitude. "You wouldn't believe how fit we are all getting!" Despite the challenges they faced with her husband's illness, they retained their good-natured humour throughout. My respect and admiration for them was reignited and I felt inspired by them once more.

However, she continued, when one family member went into the shop to get the ice cream, Luna would leap and bound and stand on her back legs, yapping and screaming and making a right scene. Even though the rest of the family were with her, she screamed her head off every time it happened and they didn't know how to stop it. It was embarrassing. She reported that it didn't matter which member of the family left to get the ice cream, Luna acted the same, screaming, barking, whirling round and jumping up on her hind legs, pulling and yanking at her lead the whole time, until the ice cream bearer returned.

This news surprised me a great deal as memories of Luna's placid calmness came flooding back from her class days. Furthermore, I clearly remembered that Luna had advanced to the point where she, together with the rest of the class, could do a two-minute down stay in one room whilst her family left her and went to another. A standard obedience exercise, this process usually highlighted dogs who couldn't cope well on their own. Luna had sailed through this exercise flawlessly. *Hmmmm.* My mind went into a whirl. Perhaps she was screaming in anticipation of the ice cream?

I really didn't know what to make of this. Remembering Luna as I did, I just couldn't think why she would behave this way. So, unable to help them on the phone, we arranged to meet near to the ice cream shop the very next day. I looked forward to seeing them all again.

So I set off with a happy heart to see the lovely family again, hoping so much that I could help them. When I arrived, they were all waiting for me, smiling and waving as I approached. The lady gave me a hug and the children all greeted me, though the husband stayed further back.

"Allergies, sorry," he explained. Whilst the family and Luna looked much as I remembered them, the husband looked weary, older, ill.

Luna wagged her tail and came to say hi to me, though she soon returned her focus to her family. She stood on a loose lead looking around in a relaxed fashion and she looked fit and well, with a shiny coat and bright eyes. She looked far better than the owner whom she made so ill.

So the time had come for me to see what Luna was doing and why, so we walked the few yards to the ice cream shop. When we arrived there, Luna seemed alert and a bit tense. Was she anticipating the moment when one of her family would leave?

Standing where they normally did, the opposite side of the road from the ice cream shop under the shade of a tree, I asked for one of them to go get the ice cream, as normal. Dad decided to be the one and Mum held the lead as she and the children watched for Luna's manic behaviour to begin.

Sure enough, as soon as the husband stepped in the direction of the shop, Luna rose up on her back legs and began to bark and scream. She fell down onto all fours again, span in a circle, leapt up again and recommenced her screaming. It continued unabated as I watched and she didn't calm down the whole time the man was absent. Scream, bark, spin, scream, bark, spin. Mum tried to distract her and reached for her collar to lessen her leaping and calm her, but Luna's leaping and screaming continued. I was genuinely shocked at the severity of Luna's agitation.

The very moment the shop door opened and the man appeared with two hands full of ice creams, she dropped to all fours and became completely silent again. She wagged her tail and returned to the happy, calm Luna that I remembered. *How odd*, I thought. But straight away, thankfully, I had an idea.

Dogs are purely logical in their thought processes. They believe that what they do influences whatever happens next. In other words, dogs think that everything they do affects everything that happens. The very first time someone had left her to go into the shop, Luna had barked and screamed and leapt about, after which the dad had returned. So Luna will have thought that her screaming had contributed to his return. From then on she thought that she had to behave this way, to get him to return.

It's common in separation anxiety in the home, too, for dogs to follow the same logic. "When I bark, howl, dig, tear things up, scream, or chew the door, they eventually return, so I must do that to get them to do so." The trick is to find a way of changing their behaviour so that they are quiet and calm when their owner returns. In this way, they learn that they must be quiet and calm for them to return.

I explained this to the family. They listened intently and then the mother smiled. "Yes, that makes sense," she said, and as I looked round I saw them all nod in agreement. They understood.

"So how," Mum asked, "do we get her to be quiet so that she can learn that being quiet would bring him back?" I loved the intelligence of this family.

Looking back at her quiet, calm behaviour in class when she was left alone in a room for two minutes, I applied the same process.

I waited until we had all finished our ice creams and then asked if the husband would mind going into the shop once again.

"It depends," he said, smiling. "Do I have to buy you all another ice cream? This dog is costing me a fortune!" and we all giggled. He had agreed to go so I asked him to turn to Luna and tell her to sit and stay before leaving, just like he used to in class. He told her to sit, and she sat. He raised his 'stay' hand and asked her to stay, just as he did in class. And then he turned and walked away. Again, just as he had in class.

Luna sat there. In silence. Waiting. Just like she had been taught to in classes all those months ago.

He entered the shop, paused for a while as I had asked him and then returned. Luna didn't budge. She neither moved nor uttered any noise. She sat as obediently and calmly as she had when she was still in class. As he came back across the road he was beaming. They were all beaming.

"Is that it? Is that all there is to it?" the mother asked.

"Yep," I beamed back at them. And that was it. Problem solved.

"Well, how about that then!" the father said, grinning again. "I think we all deserve another ice cream." He turned to Luna and said, "Sit, stay," and off he went, returning later with six more ice creams and a happy smiling face. He rewarded his dog for the silence that she had displayed with ice cream number two of this happy day.

When a dog finds itself in a novel situation, especially when there is some stress involved (perhaps a member of the family has disappeared) they have to find a way to cope. They don't know what to do. It is new to them.

The simple solution, detailed here, is the answer to preventing so many different problems – when a dog doesn't know what to do, take the stress and guesswork out of it for the dog and *tell them*! Tell the dog how you wish it to behave in each new situation as it occurs. Tell them what is wanted of them before exposing them to the new event. Luna knew what sit and stay meant. It meant what we had trained it to mean: I am going to leave you here whilst I move away for a while, but I will *always* return to you.

And so, content that sit and stay meant that the father would return, Luna could happily relax in that knowledge. She didn't have to *do* anything. She just had to wait calmly.

Simple, but effective.

After that day, I thought a lot more about the reasons that dogs get stressed when left, and I began to apply new processes to my separation anxiety cases with great success. For many dogs (though not all) that suffer separation anxiety, it can simply be a case of teaching the dog to stay on its bed for increasing lengths of time whilst the owner leaves and returns.

I tested this with my own dogs and discovered that if I take them to a friend's house and whilst there I get up and leave the room without speaking to them, they will actually stand behind the door I close and bark, presumably to tell me that I have forgotten to take them with me. If, however, I tell them to 'stay there', they accept that I have left but will return, and they do not bark. Such a simple thing, but it can work really well.

★

Thank you to Luna's lovely family for bringing not only me and the readers of this book further understanding, but also for inspiring us with your utter commitment to, and love of, your dog. It is priceless to me that there are people like you out there: people who inspire others in your own natural behaviour. Thank you.

To Luna, you have inspired us in knowing you and your family. May you wait for your ice cream in peace and relaxation, for all time.

Keep calm and eat ice cream!

"I'm a dog trainer"

I have always had a deep-rooted fear of all things medical, and of all places where medical things happen.

I think the fear probably stems from my dad's reaction to my brother's and my own various medical emergencies and routine medical processes when we were small. One of my earliest memories is of being at the dentist, and when I came out of the room after treatment I couldn't see my dad in the waiting room. Panic took me, but then a kindly receptionist came and said, "It's okay, your dad is just having a lie down in the recovery room." He had passed out at the thought of me having a tooth drilled. I too developed the tendency to simply pass out when I was overcome by fear of medical things which was often, as my poor brother suffered illness after illness throughout his entire life, before very sadly being overcome by his problems at the age of fifty.

I had received several years' worth of 'invitations' to have a cervical smear before I finally succumbed, and rather bravely decided that I really must go.

As I cautiously entered the room I was met by the friendly, smiling face of the nurse. She must have seen the tension in my face and she reassured me that all would be well: it would soon be over. But I had already started to feel panic and I sensed that a fainting episode was about to ensue. I just wanted out of there.

She instructed me to remove my trousers, lie on the bed, assume the required very undignified position, and try to relax.

Relax? Are you kidding me?

I lay on the bed, and as I felt the faintness coming I knew that lying down was my best option. I saw her prepare the metal instrument of torture (as I saw it), and slowly, rather menacingly I felt, but still smiling, she approached with the metalled hand. I remembered a horrifying film I had seen that involved the scene of a torturer doing indescribably dreadful things to an innocent victim. The gory details raged momentarily in my mind as if I were living them for real.

As she reached me and prepared to insert the dreaded instrument, presumably in an effort to take my mind off the situation, she asked me, "Do you work?"

"I'm a dog trainer," I replied.

In very theatrical style she instantly withdrew from me a metre or so, her hands, one of them still obscured by the metal object she held, raised to the sky as she looked up and cried out, "Oh, praise the Lord!" She advanced on me again, leaning in close to my face. "You surely must have been sent to me! My sister has this Staffie. A rescue, poor thing, he was so thin when she got him. Do you know anything about Staffies?"

It happens so often. If I tell people I'm a dog trainer the conversation often proceeds like this: "Oh, my mother/friend/ auntie's neighbour/a lady I met at the hairdresser's/someone I know/a bloke I was chatting to on the plane last week… has a dog and it has this problem and you might be able to help."

Sometimes I don't mind, I'm glad to help, but on some occasions, and this was one of them, it is really irritating as I'm doing, thinking or talking about something else.

"A bit," I replied, as vaguely as I could.

She stepped back away from me again and looked thoughtful as she continued, "He's a lovely dog, ever so affectionate, but just lately he has started to bark at dogs when he is out on a lead. Do you know anything about dogs that bark on a lead?"

A feeling of resignation washed over me, then a desire to run from the building which I only just managed to quell.

"A little." I again replied vaguely, hoping she would sense my lack of interest and give up asking. But instead my vagueness seemed only to enthuse her further.

"Oh excellent!" she beamed. Then putting the metal instrument down on the counter, she placed both her hands on the surface either side of her and hoisted herself up onto it, so she could sit and look down on me, and she began to tell me, in great detail and with formidable theatrical expression with her hands, all about her sister's Staffie.

To some degree the distraction had worked. I was now embroiled in thoughts not of impending doom, but instead of the nurse's sister's Staffie. But deep down I just wanted the process over and I wanted to be gone.

"It's really odd," she was saying, "one minute he is fine, with some dogs he is fine, but with some he just goes…"

She paused, and looking around for something to pick up, she spotted the metal torture device, picked it up, and then she leapt off the counter and lunged toward me as I lay still on the bed. She did a very good impression of a lunging, barking Staffie, with the metal device I feared playing the starring role of the dog's barking mouth.

I recoiled in horror, not at the imaginary Staffie, but at the sight of the metal. Close up it looked even worse than I had feared. "Woof, woof, grrrrr, woof, grrrr," she said, as she lunged and thrust the instrument at my face. She lunged then recoiled, lunged then recoiled, all the time with sound effects, over and over again. It all became too much for me and I felt first the sweat and then the swimmy feeling, and then it all went dark.

When I came to, I was being comforted by the nurse in a soothing voice and she was asking me if I felt better yet. She offered me a plastic cup of water to drink from. I sipped at it tentatively.

"I'm so sorry," she said. "I guess you must be scared of Staffies? So many people seem to be." She looked sad for a moment. "I thought with you being a dog trainer and all… Anyway, I'd best get on with my job."

She smiled again and picked up the metal and advanced on me once more. I felt the sweat, the funny sound in my ears, my head went swimmy and I was gone again. When I came round for the second time, she said, "All done!" Relief washed over me. "You are free to go."

★

Five years later I found myself back there again, having to go through the same process. Again, tension and fear riffled through me as I lay there awaiting my fate. It was not the same nurse, but she did have the same approach.

"Do you work?" she enquired as she approached me. This time I was prepared.

"I'm an undertaker," I replied. I was out of there just five minutes later.

Holly's Legacy

I love many things about dogs, but one of the things I love the most is that sometimes they bring me into contact with good people. Really good people. Not always, but often.

This was one of those times.

I was driving home from work one day, back in the days before I was a full-time dog trainer, when I still had a 'proper job', as one of my relatives had called it. I was in slow-moving traffic and I was daydreaming about my agility class that I would attend later that night, as a student, when suddenly everything changed.

Traffic was heavy and I was driving on a dual carriageway. We were, I would guess, varying between zero and 40 miles per hour, nose to tail. On the other side of the crash barrier, the two rows of traffic were moving equally slowly. Stop, start, very slow, slightly less slow, stop. If you live in England, then sadly you probably know this type of traffic well.

Then she ran out into the road.

A Golden Retriever. From the left-hand side of the carriageway she just appeared, and then she disappeared in front of a car. I braked hard and put my hazard warning lights on. She had been hit by a car a few vehicles in front and to the left of me. But then somehow she crawled from beneath that car and was hit in the face, from what I could see from my position, by the next car. And now she was in front of my thankfully stationary car; her mouth and paw bleeding, she was dragging her back legs behind her.

It had been just a few seconds and *bang, bang*, she was hit twice. As she dragged herself past my bonnet, I leapt out of my car hoping to catch her and stop her advancing under the crash barrier and over onto the next carriageway. As I reached out for her, she saw me coming. Fear was in her eyes as she redoubled her efforts, got up rather shakily on all four feet again and then ducked under the barrier.

I grabbed for her tail but just couldn't get a proper grip, and it slipped from my hand and she was back in the traffic once again.

Thankfully, the nearest oncoming vehicle had seen the incident and stopped, but the car coming up the inside of that car did not stop, and just as she had seemed to get her legs underneath her properly and was moving again it hit her hard on her left hip. She spun around and disappeared out of sight to me, but she had at least, I hoped, made it off the carriageway.

Traffic started to move on my side but two people on the other carriageway had got out of their cars, holding up the traffic, and were wondering what to do about the injured dog, who had now dragged her two back legs down a narrow dead-end lane, off to the side of the main road.

A few weeks earlier, as luck would have it, there had been roadworks on that road and as a result the crash barrier a few yards ahead of me had been removed, meaning I could cross to the other carriageway and follow the injured dog down the lane she had chosen as her escape route.

There was much beeping of horns and flashing of lights from people who had not witnessed the event as I performed the illegal driving manoeuvre (please forgive me police people,

I was trying to save a dog). But those on the other carriageway seemed to read my intent, and still holding up the traffic, they waved me safely across and pointed to where she had gone.

I drove after her down the quiet single-track lane. She was about 100 yards ahead of me, lying on her right-hand side in the middle of the road. I can see the image in my head as clearly as if it were happening now. I will always see that image.

Large spots of blood trailed behind her, smeared by the dragging of her two hind legs. When I reached her I got out of the car and talked quietly to her. Telling her it would be okay, I approached cautiously. Animals who are frightened and injured can be aggressive, wary and inclined to try to run away.

She didn't try to run away. Nor was she aggressive. She just lay there.

When I finally got to her side I could see that she had lost several teeth, it looked like her jaw may be broken, she was bleeding heavily from her red froth-filled mouth and she had scrapes and cuts on her paws. She was breathing hard, had wild, staring eyes but seemed like she had no intention of trying to get away from me.

I was not first-aid trained at that time when it came to dogs, and I had no medical kit on me, so I just sat down at her side and looked at her injuries and behaviour whilst I figured out what to do.

If I pick her up will I make things worse? What if she has a broken pelvis? Or spine? Shall I call a vet or try to get her to one? Shall I roll her onto a blanket? Should I cover her eyes to keep her calm, or, given that she did not now seem frightened by me, leave them uncovered so she could see that she had kind company with her? Could I actually lift her into the car even if I got her onto a blanket? She was a big, otherwise healthy-looking animal and I had a very bad back at that time.

She just lay there. Her nearest eye tracked me but she made no sign of fleeing or acknowledging me. Was she going to die? Should I try to stem the blood or was it stopping of its own accord? I couldn't be sure. If I pressed on her bleeding broken jaw, or her bleeding tongue, to slow the blood, would I panic her? Would she try to run away or try to bite me? Would it make things worse or better? I just didn't know.

Was she going to die? Was she going to die? Was she going to die? *Oh, please don't let her die!*

Up until that moment I remember I had no actual thoughts other than *I must help this dog.* I was just shocked – it had all happened so fast and so dramatically, I was still in 'just do it' mode.

But what to do? Her head was now in an increasing pool of blood. It looked like a scene from a horror film.

Was she going to die? Then it hit me. What if she died? I would have failed her! I would have proven my incompetence in medical situations and it would all be my fault. I owned a dog. I should have got first-aid training. All people who have a dog should get first-aid training. I knew that. I felt a stupid incompetent dog owner. There and then, I committed to getting myself trained and have since been on the three canine first-aid courses. I recommend *all* dog owners to go on one. (If you are in the UK then I recommend Rachel Bean RVN. She runs the best course I have ever been on at the time of writing!)

Please don't die, beautiful dog!

What should I do? I looked to the sky for inspiration, but none was forthcoming.

But then I heard, "Holly! Oh, God, Holly!"

I looked towards where the voice had come from to see a very old man stiffly but hurriedly dismount a bicycle and rush toward us. "Holly, oh God Holly, Holly, are you okay?" Slowly, stiffly he tried to kneel beside her. It looked a very painful action for him. Her owner?

He looked at her. His face was ashen and spoke of horror, love and disbelief all at the same time. He reached as if to put his hands on her, then withdrew them as if he had realised she was a hot stove. He must have feared hurting her, as I did. Then he went to fall onto her, hugging her, but again stopped himself. And all he kept saying was, "Holly, oh God, Holly! No, please, no, Holly, Holly, Holly, please Holly, please don't die."

It was an intensely emotional moment as I watched, first hand, a display of true and complete love of an animal by a human. I felt very humbled to be part of it.

I sat back, giving him space so that he could have a private moment to just be with his dog. And as I did, I saw the tentative wag of a slightly reddened, bloodied tail. The first sign of hope. She knew he was there, and it had given her strength.

It was a moment I will never forget. She had failed to respond to my words, but had responded to him!

Hope for her sprang up in me and suddenly I felt the need to get on with things. I took charge of the shocked and frightened man and together we got her onto a blanket and into my car. Leaving his bike behind, we drove to the nearest vet which, coincidentally, was his vet.

As I drove, he looked over his shoulder all the time and kept talking to her, telling her that everything was going to be okay. He looked so frightened, so shocked.

The vets were great and took her off to run X-rays and give IV painkillers, to stabilise her and stem the bleeding. We sat together in the waiting room for a few hours and I witnessed his suffering, his pain. As time passed we started to talk and I learnt he was living alone with Holly after the death of his wife. Holly was his world. He loved her more than anything else he had.

He also explained how it came to be that Holly was on the road that day. A few years earlier, he said, his back had begun to cause so much pain he couldn't walk far, but he discovered that he could still ride a bike without too much trouble. Determined to keep Holly fit, whatever the weather, he had started to cycle twice a day along the riverbank with Holly, so she could still meet with her friends and swim in the river. It was the highlight of the day for both of them, he said.

On this particular day, everything had started out normally. He had cycled along the riverbank, under the bridge that carried the road Holly had been injured on and to the end point of the evening walk/cycle ride. After turning around to return home, as he once again approached the bridge, Holly had seen a rabbit and had taken off after it up the steep bank towards the road. He had shouted for her but to no avail and she had disappeared from his sight. Instead of returning she must have decided to cross the road and pick up the river bank path on the other side. He was terrified that she would be killed, but unable to get himself or his bike up the steep grassy bank, he whirled into panicked action and had hurried under the bridge and along the path to a place where it split and he was able to take the fork back to the little lane where I had found Holly. It was just one of those horrid accidents.

As he talked, I studied him and decided he was not a rich man. He told me of his life and it was one committed to two things, his dog and his daughter. But he had done many other good things in his long life: he had fought in the war and saved a man's life, he had worked hard and had given greatly to many. He had his daughter's love surrounding him. He was a noble old gent, but he was now in utter anguish, over Holly. When he lost his wife to cancer, he had got Holly as his company and they had been inseparable.

I was in a good job at the time, a 'proper job' and money was no object, so I decided there and then that I would pay the bill if he could not afford it; it was all I could do to ease his suffering. He told me that that was not necessary and he joked that he was a lot richer than he looked!

The vet eventually came to talk to us and told us that though she had a broken jaw, several missing teeth and a ripped-up tongue, extensive bruising and localised swelling, there were no life-threatening injuries as far as he could tell. Though she was dragging her legs when I saw her, he thought that the bang to the hip had caused temporary nerve damage and it was looking like that damage was wholly reversible. I knew this vet and I knew he was a wise and experienced man, so relief washed over me.

Holly's owner looked upward and said, "Thank you," and then he started to cry.

Holly stayed overnight at the vet's and the next day George, her owner, called me and asked if he could take me up on the offer I'd made, to take him back to the vet's to pick up Holly. She walked out stiffly and slowly toward us, assisted by a kind vet nurse who supported her with a sling. Holly's tail began to wag when she saw George; once again he knelt slowly and stiffly down to her, and this time he did hug her gently and she pushed into him, her tail a whir of complete joy and happiness.

Once again, I felt humbled and honoured to witness such a moment of total love.

George and I argued mildly over who was going to pay the vet's bill, and despite my objections, he paid it himself.

★

Over the next few months I visited Holly and George a couple of times and I was delighted to see her make a full recovery. They were both lovely to be with: he was so wise and Holly so sweet, but what impressed me the most was the total commitment and love they had for one another. Holly's lip and tongue carried scars that told the tale of that horrid day, but to all intents and purposes, within a few months, she was back to full health again. We spoke on the phone a couple of times and he kept thanking me and thanking me, and I kept telling him it was all I could do, and life went on as normal.

Then a year or so after, I got a phone call from George's daughter. She said, "Denise, I have some very sad news that I have to share."

My heart jumped in my chest. Had one or the other died? He was such an old man when I had met him. So wise, so kind, and his dog so sweet and gentle. I didn't want to hear the next words – I didn't want to hear anything bad about either of them.

But it was even worse than I had imagined. Both George and Holly had been killed in a car accident. They had died immediately, the police had said. "They probably knew nothing about it," they had told his daughter. The driver, George's friend and neighbour who had been giving them a lift, had miraculously escaped with minor injuries. It was a freak accident and an utter fluke that anyone had survived, the police had said.

My stomach tightened in pain as I heard the news. "Oh, no! I am so very sorry. Oh, that's awful, I'm so sorry. I'm so, so sorry," was all I could think of to say.

"Oh, don't be sorry," she said. "We are all seeing it as a miracle."

A miracle, that her dad and his dog should be killed in a freak accident? What kind of miracle was that?

She went on to explain. A few weeks earlier George had been diagnosed with lung cancer and given only a short time to live. His wife had died years earlier from the same condition.

"He was such a stubborn man, he never went to the doctor's until it was too late!" she said.

Then a week later, Holly had been diagnosed with bone cancer and likewise had been given only a short survival time. She was being taken to the vet for treatment when the accident had happened.

"They both faced a painful end," his daughter said, bittersweet emotion in her voice.

Apparently, on the morning of the crash, he had rung her to say that he was getting sicker; he seemed calm and accepting of his fate, but his heart was tearing apart at the thought that Holly would be left behind if he died. He was committed that he must keep going until she had died, even though he himself was running out of strength. He had not got the heart to have her put to sleep whilst she still had some quality of life, so he had committed to keeping on going until her time had come. "Then I can die in peace," he had said.

She took a few moments to compose herself, and I waited as she did so.

"This way," she said, "he didn't leave Holly behind. Nor did she leave him. Neither could have been happy without the other. Not for a moment. We are all so thankful that it happened this way. It is a miracle!"

She paused before continuing, "Thank you for saving Holly and for caring for Dad as you have. He spoke of you often and said that without you, he would have lost Holly."

I couldn't take any credit for that. It was the vet who had saved her, not me.

"I have a cheque that I want to send to you. Dad asked me to give you the money that you paid the vet, if his estate had enough in it after he died. He was never a rich man." She giggled for a moment. "Always giving his money away to better causes!" she said. "He never stopped talking of you and saying you saved Holly's life. He said you must spend it on yourself!"

But I had never paid the vet's bill!

I told her I had not paid the bill. She knew that already, she said. But George had insisted that when he died I was to have the several hundred pounds that I had offered to pay for Holly. She was determined to make all his wishes come true so she insisted on it, and sure enough, one day shortly afterwards, the cheque arrived.

At that time, I didn't really need the money. I thought long and hard about what to do with it, but didn't arrive at any conclusion. I wondered about giving it to charity, but George had wanted me to spend it on myself, his daughter had said. I put it in the bank, and figured that one day it might come in handy.

Shortly afterwards, when I finally decided to go full time into dog training and behaviour and quit my 'proper job', I did need the money.

I wanted to spend it wisely. It was George's money and I wanted him to be proud of my choice. So I spent it on a set of agility equipment so that I could run my first ever dog-training classes as a professional.

That set of agility equipment brought happiness to hundreds of dogs and people. It brought dogs and owners closer together, it helped rehab worried, fearful dogs, it helped me get into dog training, and every time it was used, it helped another dog. I smiled inside as I watched dog after dog have fun and grow confident at agility, and I thanked George and Holly for this opportunity.

And through those dogs and owners, their legacy of love carries on. The love of one man for his dog allowed the love of other owners for their dogs to grow and develop as both learned to have fun at agility.

★

To George and Holly. Thank you for inspiring me with your love for one another. For showing me kindness and care. For giving me the money that made so many people and dogs happy. And thank you for being an inspiration, from the day I met you to the day I will meet you again.

May your love for one another live on and on.

The Dog's Nose Knows, You Know

In the early 1990s I acquired Cassie, who was to be my first agility dog, and I set out to find us a suitable trainer and a place to train. I'd seen agility on TV and at some country fairs and it looked so much fun. I'd ridden show jumpers all through my childhood and teens and I saw this as show jumping for dogs.

Cassie was eighteen months old when I picked her up from the RSPCA shelter where she had spent many months, due to her fear issues. She was terrified, and I mean *terrified*, of people. Her recovery was a slow one at first and for the first few months we focused on being able to get her out of the house and to walk down the road when other people were in sight. At the same time I took her to the stables with me and taught her all I could about jumping, climbing and taking arm signals and commands at a distance. She seemed to love it, and as a German Shepherd cross Whippet (I think) she was both fast and bright!

Slowly, she started to find things easier and when she could finally stand within a few metres of people without cowering or trying to get away, I located and went to meet my new agility instructor, Dave Blackshaw, a local guy who seemed to have got himself quite a following.

Right from day one, Cassie just did almost everything I asked of her, and there at her very first agility class she completed the whole course at full height. The see-saw freaked her out a bit and we both needed to learn how to wait on contacts and do the weaves, but apart from these things, she went clear through every round.

Not only was agility great fun for her and for me, it was also the solution to Cassie's fear – and became one of my mainstay solutions to fear in dogs that I have used many, many times since: whilst she was doing agility, she forgot all about the people who scared her! Focusing on an activity that they love can switch on the 'happy' side of a dog's brain and therefore diminish the power that fear can have. Whenever there is fear or depression or anxiety, then if at all possible I follow (and encourage others to follow) a very simple rule: whatever you love, do that!

After a few weeks, Cassie finally began to approach people in a friendly fashion, instead of cowering and trying to run away. She associated humans with the fun and feel-good factor of agility and it was both amazing and humbling to observe; for Cassie it was a breakthrough that she never looked back on. It was amazing how it happened. We had been in class about fifteen minutes when for no apparent reason, she decided to approach someone she had seen every week since attendance. The lady thankfully was kind but calm with her and as Cassie reached her nose toward her, she said, "Hi Cassie" gently, but did not move. Cassie began her recovery from fear that very moment. The moment she safely survived making contact with a human. Nothing bad had happened and she had learned that another human could be trusted. Later that night the lady offered her some food, and Cassie took it from her hand. Her recovery was underway.

I was thrilled at how well she had done that first night and Dave told me how impressed he was. I was beyond thrilled at his words and I blushed deep crimson with pride and beamed a smile inside and out for many weeks to come! Cassie was going to be a good agility dog and one of my dreams was about to come true. I was sure of it!

★

Advising me that we needed to work privately on her contact and weaves, Dave arranged a few private sessions with Cassie and I up at Agnes Meadow – a lovely, sunny place, situated high up on a hill, with stunning views and access to agility equipment seven days a week. I was in a state of total joy in this lovely place, watching Cassie grow in skill and confidence. I felt I was in the right place at the right time and I was brimming with excitement. One day soon I would be able to compete.

The private sessions went well and the third one was followed by an invitation for a beer – as is Dave's way. So off to the pub we went.

We entered the cosy country inn and Dave signalled for me to be seated. As I sat, he leaned forward to ask what I wanted to drink. "Lime and soda please," I answered, my standard daytime drink.

"Okay," he replied, and then he paused momentarily, raised his right arm and showed me his flat palm, commanding me to "Stay there"! I guessed it must be hard to not be a dog trainer, when you are a dog trainer.

It made me giggle that he should treat me like his dog and I sat and stayed obligingly. I awaited a pat on the head as a reward, or a piece of cheese, but sadly got neither!

I felt humbled and privileged to spend time with this man who knew so much about dogs and agility and who, I later discovered, was right at the very top of the agility tree. At that time, he had not one but two dogs in the top ten dogs in the UK, who were vying for pole position as agility dog of the year! He had already won hundreds of titles and awards as well as competed for the British team. What a stroke of luck – a very experienced trainer, right at the top of his agility career, and a nice fella too!

We met and trained and went to the pub several times, where I was a sponge for tales of his life with dogs and agility and obedience successes. He was friendly with some very famous names – he often camped with them at shows – and I longed to become part of that set.

Although I didn't agree with everything he said or did, I did learn a huge amount from this, my first ever dog-training instructor. He taught me how to give and receive support, how to encourage and enthuse clients, as well as their dogs. How to stay calm when one's nerves are in tatters and how to be not just an instructor, but also an entertainer and a friend to clients.

I began to dream of being just like him, training dogs for a living, competing at the highest level and being known as a good soul and a talented trainer. It sowed a seed in my mind… Maybe one day, I might be a professional dog trainer too. Just maybe…

Then I discovered that he could play the guitar really well and sing beautifully too, and suddenly, having always been attracted to musicians, I was smitten.

Soon we were more than just friends, and eventually the day came when I was to accompany Dave, world-famous dog trainer, to a show where he was judging – as his girlfriend!

I was a mishmash of uncontainable excitement and gut-wrenching nerves. Still in my twenties, I was fundamentally shy and often I was very uncomfortable around people.

Animals I mostly understood, whereas people still baffled me. But I wanted to fit in with all his friends, I wanted them to like me and I wanted to learn all I could from the dog-wise people who I knew I was about to meet. But most of all, I didn't want to make a tit of myself in front of such a famous, knowing and successful crowd.

The day dawned, and after a long drive in my car following him and his caravan we arrived on this huge, flat field that was the size of about ten rugby pitches. As we drove onto the otherwise empty showground, I noticed a huge pile of agility equipment, ring ropes and stakes. The recently mown grass smelt of summer and invited you to just sit down and pick daisies. My nerves and excitement battled with each other in my stomach.

We had arrived early to set the courses that Dave was required to judge. There was one other caravan there, and soon another arrived, this one towed by Dave's friend – yet another famous agility person who I had already met, and liked. I admired their closeness. They seemed like peas in a pod together, the friendship easy and open between them. Their jokes were not very funny, they were mostly about fish, but their efforts to amuse were, in themselves, amusing. They were like an old married couple and it was a joy to spend time with their friendly banter.

No sooner had his friend arrived than Dave, being Dave, went off to the caravan fridge to get cold beers to share on this warm day, prior to them sorting out the caravans. He offered me a cool can which I opened and drank gratefully.

No sooner had I taken a couple of swallows than I remembered why I never drank alcohol at lunchtime. My head started to spin and as I noted that the lager was strong and my tolerance extremely low, thinking that in this state I might make some kind of fool of myself, I attempted to duck out of the caravan set-up process and go off and clear my head by offering to walk the dogs.

Dave agreed, so I took my Cassie and his two dogs, Kelly and his own Cassie, and we walked on-lead across the huge field to the edge, to see what lay beyond. I knew the walk would bring me back to my senses.

We dropped down a bank at the far side of the enormous field and picked up a path through the heathland that lay beyond. I'd walked Dave's dogs before, and knowing they were responsive to me, once they could no longer see Dave, I let them off the lead. We all bounded happily downhill, hoping for water at the bottom. My nerves began to settle now that I was in my comfort zone, walking dogs, with no people around. The path went on for some miles, and over an hour later we arrived at the stream where the dogs had a paddle and a drink. I sat down for a while and enjoyed watching their fun before setting off back to the huge field that held my new boyfriend's caravan.

As I ascended the bank that led to the showground, I was confronted by a surprising and confusing sight that halted me in my tracks. Where before there had been just three caravans, now there were dozens and dozens. And to me, they *all* looked exactly the same. Some had awnings, some didn't, but apart from that, they all looked like the next one. When I had left the field earlier, Dave had been putting up his awning, so I looked just at the ones which had awnings, but it made it no clearer. Which one was Dave's? I felt anxiety rise in me. How could I find Dave's caravan without looking like an idiot, a new kid on the block, who had lost her boyfriend's caravan?

I cringed inside. I wondered what kind of sense of humour agility people had. Did they consider people who couldn't find a caravan they had just been in to be stupid? Would they laugh at me? I wondered a lot of stupid things in my paranoid state,

THE DOG'S NOSE KNOWS, YOU KNOW

but then I had a bright idea. Ping! It was obvious – Dave's dogs would be able to find him in his van! Relief flooded through me at finding such a simple solution. His dogs were used to agility shows and I already knew just how efficient a dog can be when locating its owner, as my own Cassie, months earlier, had broken out of a garden to track me down – and she found me! That was the answer. I heaved an internal sigh of relief. The dogs would take me there, I knew they would, and I would enjoy watching them succeed at their task, too. There are few finer things in life than watching a dog use its nose to good effect, so I smiled inside and my confidence began to return. This was going to be fun! As my mood improved, I steeled myself to being confronted by all of Dave's famous friends and trying not to make any more of an idiot of myself. The dogs would save me – no one need know of my foolishness.

We wandered towards the vans. Dave's Kelly and Cassie, so well trained, had been walking at my side. But I urged them forward: "Go find Dad!" They probably had no idea what I was talking about but they seemed enthused by my greater enthusiasm, and Kelly, the older dog, started to lean forward into her lead. She scented the air as she went. Success was afoot, I felt. She walked confidently up between two rows of unfamiliar vans, and then she turned abruptly, dodging two barking dogs as she did so. She continued sharp right to pass once more along two more rows of identical white boxes.

I had hoped to remain incognito whilst I floundered around in embarrassment, looking for my new weekend 'home'. But many people looked up as we walked past, no doubt recognising Dave's very well-known dogs, but failing to recognise me. My paranoia grew at the attention I was receiving: all eyes seemed to be on me.

We walked on, and after passing several dozen vans, Kelly leaned down hard into her collar. She quickened her pace for a few strides and then turned sharp left, under Dave's awning, keen to hop into the van. I released the dogs from their leads. Jumping over the caravan step, they hopped up immediately into the van and my Cassie and I stepped in behind them, relieved that at last the public ordeal was over. Phew!

But there, at the front of the van, was an athletic, tanned, half-naked woman, who was just pulling her T-shirt back over her bra! Her bare legs were honed with muscle; she looked fit and strong like a runner. She greeted Dave's dogs warmly, and they jumped up on the left-hand couch. She now stood and stared at me blankly. *What the hell is going on here?* I wondered.

I paused in the doorway to consider the situation a moment, before taking action. Perhaps she didn't have a caravan and she had borrowed the privacy of Dave's to change her clothes? Maybe she had been poorly and Dave had leant her his couch to rest on? Where was Dave anyway? The horse world I'd once been part of occasionally had some 'extra-marital events'; maybe the agility circuit was just the same? I didn't know.

I didn't want to be rude to her, but I didn't want to lose face either, so as she stared at me blankly, her presence blocking my way to the seat next to the dogs where I had hoped to sit, I stared back as impassively as I could. Though my mind was in freefall with thoughts, I wanted to stay looking cool, so I halted my tongue momentarily and hoped that inspiration would strike.

We stood there briefly in silence, eyeing one another, opposite one another, in that tiny space. She stared at me and I stared at her. Eventually, I felt the need to speak.

"Hello," I said simply. It was all I could think of. My crazed moment of hurried thinking hadn't amounted to many words.

"Hello," came her equally uninformative reply. I had been hoping for some explanation of why she was half naked in my boyfriend's caravan, but none was forthcoming.

The dogs, now comfy on the sofa, heaved a sigh as they settled for a nap after their long walk. But otherwise the tense quietness continued.

"Nice day!" I continued, trying to drown out the embarrassing silence which engulfed us both. Would she reveal more about why she was there?

"It is," she replied.

Another silence screamed at me. I looked at the seat I wanted to sit on and decided I must take action, so I stepped toward it. But she was standing in the way so I had to use spatial pressure and intent to back her up against the front of the van somewhat, so that I could reach the welcoming sofa. I was skilled at spatial pressure. I had rounded up many flocks of sheep and herds of cows during my time, so I knew the impact that body positioning can have. As long as someone isn't angry, it is actually quite easy to back them up slightly, without touching them or saying anything. So I backed her up with my own body presence, pushing her backwards further to the edge of the little room we now shared. It created the gap I needed to reach the seat I so badly wanted.

She read my intent and stepped back out of the way so that I could sit. I sat down next to the dogs and my Cassie came and sat between my legs. The woman continued to stare at me, but got dressed at the same time. At least she had her clothes on now.

I wanted to 'own' this space, my boyfriend's caravan, so I took off my shoes and socks, and swinging my legs up and over Kelly, I made myself at home, to prove a point. The silence was getting louder and my heart was now racing. Why was this woman still here? Why had she got so few clothes on? Why did she know Dave's dogs so well? And where was Dave? I was getting very anxious and I felt I needed answers, quickly.

All of a sudden I felt the need for a bit of normality – I felt the need for a cup of tea. Tea: that very British solution to a myriad of wrongs. I looked over at the kettle which was on the stove, and realised that to boil it, I had to again pass the stranger in the narrow caravan.

I went for the classic ice breaker: "Do you want a cup of tea?" Maybe over tea, she might spill the beans about who she was and why she was there.

"No thanks." She cut off that option.

And then I had a sudden uncomfortable feeling. I looked back at the stove again. I shifted uneasily in my seat as my stomach turned over with embarrassment. Dave's stove was at the back of his van. This one was in the middle. This was *not* Dave's van!

Feeling like I'd been kicked in the guts, embarrassment engulfed me as I wondered how I could get out of this situation without making even more of an idiot of myself.

She must have read my feelings from my face and taken pity on me. "Are you looking for Dave, by any chance?" She nodded at Dave's dogs, as if to inform me how she knew I was looking for Dave.

"Er, yes, do you know where he is?"

"Maybe in his *own* van?" She smiled at me and the tension eased slightly.

There was no way to look cool any longer; I just had to go with the flow of things.

"Oh, do you happen to know where that is?" I enquired, cringing at my own stupidity.

"Yes, it's three vans down that way." She pointed to the back of her van. "It has *his* silver-blue car outside of it, rather than my black four-by-four!" Again I detected a smile. But she wasn't mocking me, she was merely amused. Then she continued, "The car at the side of Dave's, I assume, is yours?"

Immediately I realised how stupid I had been – Dave's car would be parked next to my own car! Why had I not just gone in search of my own car? The excitement and nerves must have clouded my judgment.

"Oh yes, of course. Thank you," I replied, as if nothing odd had occurred. "Thank you for your help."

I should have then kept my mouth shut and exited with my dignity relatively intact, but I didn't. Trying to be polite, I continued, "Please do help yourself to a cup of tea." I gestured to her own kettle. *Whatever possessed me?*

Calling the dogs, I hastened my retreat.

When I told Dave of my cringe-worthy experience, he laughed so hard that I thought he might crack open. His friend too found great delight in my humiliating faux pas. I felt like getting in my car to drive away from agility forever. But I wanted to be there so much that I steeled myself, and I stayed.

★

Later that night, as Dave and I entered the rugby team's clubhouse, a huge round of applause erupted.

"You managed to find your way here, then!" came a voice I didn't know. Everyone, it seemed, knew of my embarrassing mistake and as I felt the flush of blood to my cheeks, I knew I had a long way to go to recover my 'cool' on the agility circuit. Not the start I had been hoping for!

But in reality, as time would tell, I didn't have to recover my cool. For in just a few weeks' time, my dog Cassie was about to recover that cool for me when she came fifth in her first ever agility class, open agility at Rugby show, then one of the very biggest of all shows.

To receive her award, she stood in the line-up, and behind her, lower placed in the results, were not just Dave and his equally talented friend, but other famous names that I recognised too! In those days, this was an incredible achievement for a non-Border Collie.

At her first twelve shows she won or was placed in virtually every class she was entered into. She was running in finals just a few months later, and for a while she headed up the *Agility Voice* scoreboard for the leader of Novice Dog of the Year competition, which was based on points accumulated via wins over twelve months.

Later, when Dave was too ill to handle her, I had to handle his best dog, his 'Just Cassie', in the senior finals at Malvern show. Although we gained faults for missing a contact point, we managed to gain enough points so that she could go on to win the much-acclaimed title of Agility Dog of the Year!

It was a wonderful time that was sadly so short lived, as only a year or so later my beloved Cassie was diagnosed with dysplasia in her left hip and her agility career came to a very abrupt halt.

Around the same time, Dave cashed in his girlfriend for a newer, younger model, and I was thrown out of his club by the replacement girlfriend. But Dave and I remained firm friends and have given great support to one another ever since.

By now I had acquired another shelter dog, also great at agility, Lace, and I was determined to stay in agility despite no longer having Cassie to work and not being able to train with Dave.

With very few agility clubs to choose from back in those days, I felt I had no choice but to get two sets of agility equipment made by a local joiner, using the money that had been left to me by Holly's owner George (see previous chapter). I got myself a venue, ran a big advert in the newspaper for agility classes, was inundated with enquiries, and lo and behold just two years after starting agility, with my name now known because of Cassie's success, I was suddenly an agility instructor, and well on my way to being a professional dog trainer!

And so it had begun...

★

To my darling Cassie. Thank you for regaining my 'cool' and for giving me the love and commitment of a truly awesome best friend. I hope that wherever you are and whatever you are doing that you are pain-free and running and jumping like the 'gazelle' you once were. You trusted me and taught me so much about fear in dogs and how to push on through it, and you brought to me the very beginnings of all that has happened to me since.

Run free, and jump high, my best girl. You were, and always will be, my number one dog. May we run again together one day. You live on forever, in my heart.

To my dear friend Dave. You were my first instructor and arguably the best (though your jokes were definitely the worst). You instilled in me confidence, self-belief and a great number of skills for which I will always be grateful. Skills that I have since adopted in my role as instructor. I have chosen, though, not to borrow your fish jokes.

I send you 1,000 thank yous for all you did back then, and all that you have done since then, for me. You are a rum bugger, but also a true gent with a giving and generous heart of gold.

Thank you, Dave!

Attack!

This is not the story of a case dog, but instead a story about a friend's dog. A little dog that I have come to know and love very much, who belongs to a good friend of ours, Mark.

As I heard the phone ring, I looked at the display and saw it was my friend calling. Expecting it to be just a social call, I was surprised when immediately a voice filled with grave concern reached my ear.

"It's Bruce, Dee. He's… well, he's… been attacked!"

His worry was tangible, almost as if he didn't want to say the words, didn't want to believe it himself. Bruce is a small Chihuahua crossed with a Jack Russell, and he weighs just a few pounds. Most of his bodyweight, it seems to me, is made up of his testicles.

At the time of the attack he was around six years old. Bruce and his owner often walked with us and sometimes we all went on holiday together, so the dogs all got on very well. Mine accepted the little dog into the 'holiday group' as if he was a forever friend. Both Simon and I had grown very fond indeed of little Bruce. 'Ballsy Bruce' we called him, on account of both his large testicles and his plucky attitude.

Mark continued, "We were away on holiday and this big mastiff dog grabbed him by the head, lifted him off the ground and shook him from side to side, over and over again. It was terrible, Dee. He was screaming and I thought he would be killed. One minute it looked like they were making friends and then the dog just grabbed him."

I saw little Bruce in my mind being shaken around by a dog so huge that it could easily have chomped Bruce's tiny skull flat. I felt a churning in my stomach and I dreaded what words I might hear next. I sat down as I felt my knees weaken. Poor Brucie!

Bruce was normally a good-natured little fella who wore the attitude of wanting to be friends with all dogs, but with the understandable caution of a dog who was very small and living in a world full of much bigger dogs. He would duck and dive and skip out of the way when the bigger dogs ran around him or ran near him, and if anyone was in danger of not noticing him, or failing to take care around him, he would use a short mock charge and a lot of little barks to get bigger dogs to pay attention to their own movements and take more care not to tread on him. He was a good life lesson for them and in turn, they for him. But when he was crossed or worried by the bigger dogs' active behaviour, for a moment he would appear like a little demon, all teeth and snarling and barking, for just a few seconds, before returning to his normal friendly and polite attitude to them. I had never seen him be really nasty with my dogs or any other dogs, so I doubted very much if he had deserved the beating he appeared to have taken from this powerful individual. My heart went out to him and his very worried owner, who soon continued the tale.

Mark went on to explain that Bruce had suffered severe injuries, with deep punctures and extensive lacerations around his head, neck and shoulders. He had been treated by a vet and had many stitches and drains in place. Mark sounded so concerned. But he had rung to ask for my advice, not my sympathy.

The incident had occurred a few days earlier and since that time Bruce had been very quiet. He was making it out into the garden to toilet once a day but apart from that he was worryingly withdrawn, just sleeping, or lying on his bed. He had not really left his bed but for the once daily toilet outing and he appeared aloof and distant with Mark and not very interested in eating or drinking. He was still under the care of the vet and was due to go back for a check-up the following day.

"Is it normal for him to be so quiet?" he asked me.

I assured him that animals on the whole tended to adopt this 'I'm not doing anything but existing, I need to sleep and rest' attitude to both severe shocks and illness and early recovery. That he had eaten at all was a good sign even if it had been only a little cooked chicken and mince that had finally tempted him. Although his injuries sounded horrific, and required ongoing veterinary treatment, it did sound like he was likely to survive. I felt relief flood through me.

Mark quizzed me as to the best way to approach his re-introduction to dogs, once he was well enough and enthused enough to venture out into the world again.

*

Specialising as I do in aggression and reactivity, sadly I have many phone calls about dogs who have been attacked by other dogs – owners asking me, "What should I do to get him over it?"

Over the years, I have come to see specific patterns of behaviour following dog-on-dog attacks. Where the dog previously had good social skills and had other dog friends, in almost all cases where an owner has taken the approach of 'let's get back to normal as soon as possible', and taken their dog out to mix with other dogs soon after the event, then the dog in question usually just got on with it too, with little or no change to their own view of or behaviour towards other dogs. They seem to have an inherent understanding that, in most cases, being attacked by one dog doesn't necessarily mean that from this moment on, all dogs would attack them. In the majority of cases they most often seem to recover from attacks a lot easier than their owners! Though there are always exceptions to that and every other rule.

Sometimes though, taking them out and about immediately isn't possible, such as if they are sick, like Bruce. Also, sometimes it isn't possible because their owner has lost the courage to mix their dog with others. And I can totally understand and respect that approach: they want to keep their dog safe.

Quite understandably, many owners are so horrified by the sight of their dog being attacked, that they themselves carry the trauma around in their heads for a lot longer than the dog itself does. They relive the memory over and over again, and the mental and emotional anguish that goes with it, thereby keeping the memory alive.

It is interesting to note that the human body experiences almost the exact same symptoms when we recall a shocking or painful event as it does when such an event actually happens. People are sometimes utterly overwhelmed with emotion when they remember something bad, almost as if it were happening all over again. Every time Mark, and other owners who've had similarly horrible experiences, relive the event in their mind, they also experience great emotional pain with it.

Dogs generally don't appear to do that. Dogs appear to prefer to play ball, or hunt small things, pee up car wheels, play with their friends, swim in the lake, track down that bitch that's in heat, just run around in circles because they can, compete in agility or obedience, roll joyously in fox poo, stand next to their owner and shake off water from their coat, bark at the postman, chew on a bone, or do anything else that they like to do. They prefer to get on with life and enjoy what they are doing right now, whereas many humans dwell in the past, sometimes for a long time into the future. But once again there are exceptions.

I have seen so many owners who have witnessed an attack on their own dog change their behaviour or normal behaviour patterns, or act in such a worried way next time their dog encounters another dog that it can appear as if it were *they* that got attacked. An attack can sometimes be the starting point for on-leash reactivity, as the worried owner begins to tense up when they see an oncoming strange dog and tighten the leash, or behave in an anxious way as they expect their dog to be frightened.

On an observational level, it seems to me that animals strive most often to be free of trauma when they are given the opportunity to free themselves, whereas some people seem to cling to it, knowingly or sometimes not knowingly, consciously, or sometimes unconsciously, as if it has redefined them permanently.

This is totally understandable. The owner has most often made a commitment to themselves unconsciously to keep their dog safe and well. They feel pain when they see their dog in pain. They feel fear when they see their dog in fear. Additionally, in the event of an attack they can feel as if they've failed their dog or have been a careless owner. So they feel guilt. Sometimes they *have* been a careless owner, and the incident draws attention to their lack of care-giving, but most often, it is just one of those things that happens from time to time, to dogs and their owners. All of us have bad dog incidents some days.

If you drive a car, the chances are that at some point you're likely to come into conflict or even physical combat with other drivers. If you push a shopping trolley around a supermarket then the chances are you're likely to come into conflict at some point with other shopping trolley users. But hopefully that will not stop you from shopping or driving.

Many times, people have called me to say their dog has been attacked and what should they do, and my answer is always the same. Once the dog is well enough to do so physically, get him back out into the world, finding some friendly, mature dogs to mix with, his existing friends if he has any being a great starting point. Begin to live life just as you did before the attack. Dogs get over things, usually very easily. I ask them to get back in touch with me if the dog doesn't return completely to normal very quickly. Sometimes I walk with them with my dogs so they can see their dog in relaxed, friendly company and regain any confidence which may have been lost from both dog and owner.

★

Mark was reassured that his thinking and mine were in a similar vein and he committed to get Bruce out and about as soon as he was strong and well enough. We concluded the conversation and I asked him to keep me informed on the little dog's progress.

I was kept informed by text, and was pleased to hear that after seven days of almost complete stillness, Bruce started to show more interest in things; slowly he began eating and drinking more normally and Mark was ready to start taking him out for short walks.

Then another phone call came. Again, I heard real distress and worry in his voice.

"He hates me, Dee."

There was a long pause.

"He blames me, I know he does, and I don't know what to do. He just won't let me near him. It's so upsetting to see. He is frightened of me, I know it. I can't get him out for a walk as he won't let me put his lead on. He is hiding away and when I try to get him, he backs away and he looks so scared. He hates me. What shall I do now?"

I detected a deep sadness in his tone. Once again my heart wrenched itself seemingly a few inches across my chest.

Before answering him, in my mind, I revisited the information I had already received from Mark about the original incident, searching for reasons for and solutions to this new problem – Bruce being afraid of his once-loved best friend and owner. Prior to this event, Bruce had doted on his owner, they had done everything together and it looked from the outside like man and dog at complete peace with one another. Now Bruce wouldn't let him near him and all affection towards his owner appeared to have dissolved, as Bruce continuously sought alone time.

At the time of the original attack, Mark had managed to wrestle open the jaws of the much larger mastiff, no doubt saving Bruce's life, and bleeding heavily, Bruce had dropped to the ground and had immediately scuttled away underneath Mark's motorhome seeking safety and refuge. Realising Bruce needed an immediate closer inspection and most probably medical attention, Mark had tried and tried to get him out from there, calling him, beckoning him, trying to tempt him out with bits of tasty food so that he could stem the bleeding and seek proper veterinary care.

Mark had got down and crawled under the van to retrieve Bruce, calling gently to his best friend, wanting to help him, to keep him alive. But the little dog, frightened and shaking, had skulked away, evading his grasp. Blood trailed behind his every move. Beside himself with worry that the dog might bleed to death, and realising that he was losing precious time as the bleeding continued, Mark had decided he must act fast. He had asked a friend to use a broom to stop Bruce from evading him and once again he had crawled under the van to capture the frightened, badly injured little dog. Eventually, with Bruce pinned between the motorhome wheel and the broom, unable to evade capture, Mark had reached his now further terrified little friend and had gently lifted him out from under the van to inspect the terrible wounds he had suffered. And in so doing this caring and correct act, he unwittingly damaged the bond of trust and set up a new pattern of behaviour in Bruce.

We all have somewhat unconscious patterns of behaviour. You have them, I have them and our dogs have them. These patterns or habits can be as simple as what we order when we have a takeaway, how fast we drive our car or bike around corners, to how we approach and deal with strangers; whether we smile, ignore them, or greet them cheerily. Do we shake hands, hug or bow? These are all behaviour patterns, coping mechanisms that we have adopted and maintained because they are safe and have been successful in meeting our needs. *So far.*

Prior to the incident, Bruce had a behaviour pattern of sitting with or next to his owner, often keen for contact and enjoying affection from him. Additionally when his owner called, Bruce would go to him – he had good 'recall'. Immediately after the incident, Bruce developed a new habit of avoiding Mark, and in the first days of recovery, staying away from Mark altogether, instead resting on his new 'recovery bed' close to the ground. Mark had seen his dog's reluctance to interact and had rightly respected it, realising that the little dog was in pain and allowing him the time he needed to work things out in his own head, and allow his body to heal, unimpeded by an owner's needs. But Bruce hadn't worked things out in his head how Mark had liked, nor how was best for them both.

I considered the case some more, trying to find a solution. Not only had Bruce been subjected to a probably terrifying, certainly painful and very surprising attack, he had also had his head inside the mastiff's mouth from where he could see nothing. He had no visual image to associate with the pain and the feelings. Having fled under the motorhome, the next thing he saw from under the van (after the mastiff had been removed from the scene by very apologetic owners) was Mark advancing on him.

Had Bruce linked Mark, his beloved owner, with the cause of his pain and misfortune? Did he blame him? Did he truly fear him? Had the image of his owner crawling towards him at a time he wanted to feel alone and safe caused this? I didn't really know. We could never really know unless Bruce learned to talk or write, which seemed unlikely. I could ask a million questions about the situation and conclude a million answers and I still wouldn't know for sure.

But it seemed to me that from that moment forward, their friendship was destined for trouble. Bruce wanted to stay away from Mark as he trusted him less and was wary of him. Mark wanted to draw closer to the little dog who he had thought might die. The owner wanted to comfort him and stroke him, but the dog wanted him to go away. In his loving efforts to rebuild the bond, Mark had gone on to try to coax his dog with food and the promise of playtime with toys to get him to come closer. But Bruce had evaded all his attempts and just grew more suspicious.

Furthermore, because Bruce was receiving ongoing veterinary care, Mark had had to physically drag him out of his hidey hole to take him to the vet! Bruce hated vets. So this compounded Bruce's distrust even further.

"So what shall I do, Dee?"

I had been thinking too long, and Mark had grown impatient. I'd forgotten he was on the phone... I'd drifted off to a place where I hoped I might find an answer.

What to do, what to do, what to do...?

We needed to change the pattern of behaviour. We needed to get Bruce out of thinking and behaving as if 'Dad is being weird, he keeps grabbing me when I want to be left alone and it's his fault', back to thinking, 'I want to be with my dad', owner, friend, or whatever it is that dogs see us owners as...

When any owner asks for help resolving any behaviour problem in their dog, at a very basic level there are only two possible approaches to changing that behaviour pattern:

Halt the unwanted behaviour (if possible) and create and invoke a brand new and healthier behaviour pattern.

Halt the unwanted behaviour (if possible) and identify an old behaviour pattern that is healthy, and re-invoke that.

Whether it is possible to first halt the unwanted behaviour pattern or not, the first and most commonly used way *is to identify a healthy and desirable new behaviour pattern and train the dog to do that, instead of the unwanted one.* For example, to stop a dog jumping up at visitors (old pattern), we might first make the jumping up undesirable and then we *could* teach the dog to instead go lie on its bed (new pattern) or sit patiently when visitors arrive and reward that. That would be establishing a new pattern and promoting that over and above the jumping-up pattern.

Training in a new behaviour was not an option for Bruce, as he was currently unresponsive to normal training. He wasn't tempted with affection, food or toys and he was fearful of Mark's attention: he was in avoidance mode. Not a good place to start training.

The other possible approach is to do something that *invokes an old behaviour pattern* that is still healthy. In Bruce's case this meant we needed to reignite the behaviour patterns that he *used* to display towards Mark, before the attack. We needed to take his behaviour back in time. In some cases, and certainly in Bruce's, this is the only choice.

What this essentially means is we need to get Mark back to doing what he used to do before the attack and in so doing, hope that Mark's behaviour changes from 'worried, ever-present nursemaid/Dad' to 'Dad of old' would trigger Bruce's former feelings and behaviours.

"So what should I do Dee?... Dee, are you still there?"

I'd forgotten him again. Frustration had raised his voice nearly an octave, so I thought I'd better say something.

"Go out Mark. Go out in the car and leave him at home, alone. Make sure he has all he needs and has had a chance to toilet, to eat and drink, then go out," I replied.

To Mark this must have sounded counter-intuitive – go out and leave the sick, worried dog all alone.

There was a brief silence at the end of the phone. Then came a confused reply.

"Go out? You want me to go out and leave him all alone? He is still poorly Dee, he needs me right now!" He sounded surprised and rather dismayed.

I tried to explain. "He is now in recovery and you both need things to get back to normal. You need to try this Mark, and if it doesn't work, we'll come up with another plan."

I had no idea what else we could try if this failed. I crossed my fingers and put them behind my back, an unconscious act from childhood. An act of hope.

"Yes, go out and leave him." I continued, "Please Mark, just trust me on this one, please try it. We need for him to think and feel as he used to, before the incident."

There was a brief silence at the end of the phone as he absorbed what I had said.

"I don't think I'll feel comfortable leaving him whilst he is like this, Dee. Are you sure this is the right thing to do?" He sounded doubtful and even more worried.

I could never be 100 per cent sure about anything, but I couldn't think what else to do, so I faked my own conviction to give Mark the confidence to do it.

"Yes. I'm sure. Please do it Mark and let me know how it goes."

The conversation concluded. Mark no doubt remained dubious and even I wasn't sure. I realised that my fingers were hurting, so I uncrossed them, and handed the outcome over to the universe.

★

Very reluctantly, Mark did go out and leave Bruce alone at home.

Whilst he was gone, Bruce no doubt went through a familiar pattern of realising he was alone. Being social, many dogs, and certainly this one, dislike being left alone. So a half hour later, when his owner returned, Bruce heard the car arrive and no doubt experienced old familiar emotions that drive the behaviour of greeting ('Dad's here! It's his car!') and when Mark stepped through the door, instead of being hidden behind the sofa, Bruce was there, behind the door, wagging his tail and waiting to see his friend and owner again.

Mark later reported that he had smiled joyously as Bruce circled happily and wagged his tail in greeting. He felt such a rush of joy as his little dog seemed pleased to see him for the first time in many days. Such relief. They shared the ritual of greeting that Mark, and Bruce too, had missed so much.

He reached down to the little dog he loved and stroked him and greeted him, and with familiar words and touches their friendship, trust and relationship began to be restored.

Old habits die hard. Something worth remembering.

It took a few more 'leaving him at home' efforts to change Bruce's mind completely about how he felt towards his owner. But inside one week, Bruce and Mark were best friends again.

Simple, effective and fast.

These days, it is not apparent, even to me, that there were ever any hard feelings between Dad and 'Ballsy Bruce' at all. Their friendship is complete and trust is fully restored.

Absence, in some cases, really does make the heart grow fonder.

And so, Ballsy Bruce is now back to full health. His behaviour towards dogs is completely unchanged from before the incident. He is a well-socialised animal with several dog friends and Mark got him out and about as soon as he was well enough. He mixed with my dogs, who were all kind and gentle with him and Bruce seemed to have no ill-effects at all lingering after the awful attack.

Mark, on the other hand, will no doubt forever carry the image of his little dog being shaken nearly to death in his mind. But he took my advice, and he acted correctly and bravely to help his little dog back to full mental and physical health. And it is great to see them now, all happy and reunited, Bruce wagging his tail and Mark smiling down at the little dog he clearly loves so much.

'The Balls' are back in town!

It's Not My Dog!

The first night of any new dog-training course is always an adventure. New puppies, dogs and owners stream into the building to face their first dog-training class together. Many of the owners we have already met before at our dog-free introduction night, the 'It's a Dog's Life' talk where I discuss preventing common behavioural problems like jumping up, chewing, mouthing, barking, and recall failures, and the importance of good nutrition, vet care, and many other things. It's a wonderful night of fun and learning and always brings light-bulb moments to owners and trainers alike.

But until week one of the new course, we have yet to meet the dogs and puppies that we are to work with. Sometimes owners are not able to attend the introduction night and in this case, when an owner arrives in class, it can be the first time we have met them too. It is usually the first time we have a chance to understand the owner's personality, the dog's personality and the unique relationship between them that will be at least partially unlike any other we have ever met. This is the story of one such lady and her dog.

★

I was sitting at the desk ticking people and dogs off as they arrived, checking vaccination cards and waiting for the class sheets to show that everyone had arrived safely. As I sat there, I heard the familiar yipping and barking outside the front door that represents the first week of the course, some children giggling and a lot of people oohing and aahing at other people's dogs. Through the propped-open door dividing the two rooms, from reception I heard what sounded like a youngish couple having stern words with one another about something. This particular night was the start of a training course for beginner adult dogs. Whenever possible, we separate our classes into dogs' age groups, if we have the space to do so.

Adult beginner-level courses tend to be filled by dogs who have been recently purchased from re-homing centres, often with unknown backgrounds, or dogs that have been found, dogs who have recently started to present behavioural problems, changed owners within a family, need appropriate socialisation or have somehow found themselves being acquired by new owners later in their life. Sometimes there are also dogs who have been with their owners since they were puppies, but have recently started to present with 'problems'. It is always an adventure receiving these older, often totally untrained dogs into our classes and we never know quite what is going to walk through the door.

As I checked my class registration sheet to see who was still to arrive, I heard a noise that was unusual at our classes. It was the tap, tap, tap of heeled shoes. I looked up to see a tall, rather elegant, older but miserable-looking lady approach the desk holding a vaccination card in one hand and in the other, a lead which had on the end of it a small, very happy-looking Jack Russell. Whilst the small dog danced and wagged continuously, looking up all the while at the lady, wanting to connect with her, she wore one of the sternest looks I had ever seen. Her well-groomed face was still attractive and she carried herself with elegance and poise, but her ageing skin had a lifetime of unhappiness seemingly etched all over it.

The dog was trotting politely at her side looking up at her. His undocked tail, held high over his back, whirled round and round and from side to side, hitting his own flank with vigour at each movement. Whilst the dog looked a lovely, delightful animal, the woman seemed uncomfortable and rather out of place with her heeled shoes, her expensive-looking ironed-with-a-centre-crease trousers and her flowery blouse buttoned to the top. On her face she wore a look as if one had suddenly and unexpectedly found oneself floundering in a huge tank filled with cow dung. She looked around her with evident distaste, as if she felt the building itself might somehow infect her with something nasty.

The dog looked like he didn't care where he was as long as he was at the side of his owner. As she reached the desk my eyes met hers and I said, "Hello, what's your dog's name please?"

It was a busy night with all the new arrivals and I was doing more than one thing at once, but her reply caught me completely by surprise and attracted my total attention.

"Oh, it's not my dog. *I hate dogs!*" She spat the words out and looked perplexed, angry even, as she answered the question. She glanced down at the attentive, wagging dog at her side and sneered at him. The dog seemed unfazed by the lack of affection being directed at him and continued to stare at her adoringly, completely oblivious to the dogs and people around him.

Surprised, I put down my pen, looked directly at her and asked, "Well, whose dog is it then?"

For a moment she bore a wistful look, but then her face contorted once more into something like anger as she answered.

"He is – or was – my friend's dog. She died a few weeks back and she asked *me* to take care of Patch when she died. She knew I hated Patch, well I hate all dogs, but she insisted and as there was no one else to do it, I thought I'd better… well, do what she wanted. It was her dying wish." She sounded angry and bitter. Perhaps she was still grieving the loss of her friend. Grief can do strange things to a person, I know.

This was a new situation for me and I was not sure what to say. "Oh, I see" was all I managed.

I checked in Patch and his owner on the registration form and then asked her to take a seat and said I hoped she enjoyed the evening. She looked at me like I'd just asked her to enjoy cleaning out a sewer using only her tongue. Then she began to walk off, but turned back to me and concluded by saying, "She said she thought Patch would 'do me some good'." She rolled her eyes and raised her eyebrows in disbelief as if I would understand her point of view completely. Then she turned and walked away, with Patch trotting on a loose lead, still looking up at her adoringly, tail wagging like mad over his back. I felt the sadness and anger that had surrounded her leave me as she moved away, and I hoped in my heart that Patch would indeed do her some good. I was glad at that moment that dogs can't understand English until taught, and hoped that the sweet little dog who had stared at her so adoringly had not understood what his new owner had said. I watched them cross the room and I felt perplexed. I had an owner in class who hated dogs, and a dog who was seemingly desperate to bond with the new owner that 'hated' him. It was going to be one of *those* nights. One to remember.

Many dogs, though not all, have an instinctive drive to bond with a human. Most humans have it too, most of us seek a partner or a friend or a group to belong to. Not all, but most. Why do we do it? Because something inside of us tells us to.

It is a powerful motivation to fulfil if you are one such dog, and I have seen some dogs behaving in an extraordinary way in an effort to attract and keep someone that they wish to bond with. Just like a young human admirer might court a would-be mate, so dogs can do the same with humans.

Sometimes people call it the honeymoon period. It usually lasts around two weeks but can be as short as a few days or even hours, or as long as many months. But sooner or later, once the relationship's rules, boundaries, roles that need fulfilling (guard dog, watch dog, companion animal, working animal) are established, the dog might then change. Sometimes it changes dramatically. A past history of aggression might suddenly reappear after a period of suppression by the dog, or a tendency to snap at dogs or people might suddenly appear, or it might be that the dog suddenly decides it's going to go upstairs after spending two weeks downstairs as instructed. Or a battle over rights to the sofa might suddenly ensue. Often this can be an old behaviour from a previous home that has been suppressed and then re-emerges, though sometimes it is a new behaviour born of its new environmental influences, or what the dog perceives as its role within its new household.

As I watched Patch from across the room I wondered if this massive effort he was making was the real Patch or the 'honeymoon' version of Patch. Something told me that this was the real Patch. No dog could act to be that attentive or sweet if it wasn't in his nature. Could it?

As the night wore on it became apparent that whilst she disliked the dog, she was determined that he would be well-behaved. She worked hard at the exercises and though she never spoke a kind word to Patch, he was so keen to please that he did all he could to understand what she was asking of him. He just seemed pleased that she was talking to him, even if each of her words were filled with semi-suppressed venom as she shouted out commands like 'sit' and 'stay' with an anger that belied the success that she had with her approach.

Of all breeds, Jack Russells are up there as one of the most commonly brought in to my behaviour sessions with problems. From my experience, some of the most aggressive and challenging of dogs are not the big breeds but these often tenacious and determined little animals, bred originally and still bred by some specifically to kill things. But Patch was at the other extreme as some Jack Russells can be; he was just one of those delightful animals that seemed happy no matter what. It was soon clear that Patch had already been well trained and was in the wrong class. This was a beginner owner but not, it seemed, a beginner-level dog. At the end of the night I asked if she could move classes to the next level up as I explained that Patch was too advanced for this level.

"If you want me to," she said dismissively, and she left the building without further words. Her feet made the tap, tap, tap noise and she was gone, heels and all.

The following week Patch returned, and this time I noted that his new owner had had a change of clothes. Gone were the heels to be replaced by a set of trainers, far more suited to our floor and dog training. Gone were the ironed-with-a-centre-crease smart trousers to be replaced by an equally smart and still expensive-looking but far more useful set of walking trousers.

Still looking very unhappy, she checked in at our registration desk without speaking to me, but instead pointing with her finger at her own name on the sheet, and turned and walked away to sit down. She had joined an established class of committed dogs and owners on their third course. The previous week they had been learning tricks. Tricks are a great way to get owners to understand their dogs better. For some reason, owners tend to find the teaching of tricks to be a lot easier than that of obedience commands, though in many cases tricks are actually more complex in their teaching and execution than training perhaps 'sit' or 'stay'. Most owners seem to engage in a much more friendly and relaxed way with their dogs if they are teaching a trick rather than obedience. We discovered this many years ago and adopted tricks as one of the best ways to teach obedience. For example, we changed 'heel' into 'twirl' but would end up at heel as just one way of making a boring task fun. Wherever possible we try to use tricks to also get people to understand just how clever dogs are; just how inventive they can be, and just how much fun teaching a dog can be. It doesn't have to be time-consuming and boring, it can be fun and enlightening. Once they get that, then they can come on in leaps and bounds.

We got to the bit of class where I asked owners to demonstrate some of the tricks that they had been working on.

As they did so, I saw for the first time Patch's owner's sour face change a little as she tried hard to hold back a smile when little Suzy, a fluffy, cute bundle of energy, weaved in and out of her owner's legs, wagging her tail like mad and jumping up and down on the spot joyously when her owner praised her. Suzy looked so happy that the whole class was smiling and clapping. Whilst Patch's owner watched Suzy, Patch just watched his owner, staring straight at her the whole time, his tail wagging furiously without a break. I wondered suddenly whether at the end of each day, the tail belonging to such a happy dog as Patch ached with tiredness.

I got the whole class up on the floor and we started to work some more on the tricks they had started the week before. I went to Patch's owner to ask her which of the tricks she most liked and would like to teach him. She chose the leg weave, so I started to demonstrate how to start the behaviour and having observed her then make the first few tentative steps toward achieving her goal, I walked away to help other students with their own tasks. But I kept an eye on Patch and his owner to make sure things were going well. Her sadness and anger worried me; I wanted her to succeed and start to enjoy the delightful dog which she had been given.

At one point I saw that Patch in his enthusiasm had whirled through her legs and then spun round and round the one leg in an effort to interpret what his rather ham-fisted owner was trying to teach him. All of a sudden things took a dramatic turn as he caught her by surprise; as she moved one foot, he had inadvertently positioned himself in the way of the foot she held mid-air and needed to place on the floor to balance. She began to fall and her only option was to stand on Patch to regain her balance. Patch tried to avoid the oncoming foot but it all happened so fast that he wasn't able to get out of the way quickly enough. I saw the fall about to happen and broke into a run across the room, in an effort to prevent her from hitting the floor, but it was too late – she had stood on Patch. He made a very loud high-pitched squeal as she came down on his front paw, followed by a moment that made me smile, inside and out.

Realising she had hurt him, her face contorted in sorrow and she said, "Oh, Patch, I'm so sorry," and for the first time since I had seen them together she bent down to touch Patch. Patch wasn't really hurt, he had just squealed in surprise more than pain I suspected, but he was suddenly overjoyed at the new attention he was receiving and he began to bounce up and down in the way of a dog who wanted to jump up at his owner, but had been taught not to. As his front paws left the floor and then came down again, in a recurring bounce, she looked at him and then she smiled and said again, "Oh Patch, I am so sorry."

My heart skipped a beat in delight. *Yes! We were there!* She felt sorry for the dog, so she must therefore be starting to like him? It had only been two weeks but already Patch and the other class dogs were making headway into her cold heart.

She looked across the room at me as I advanced on her, then she said rather apologetically, "I stood on him, it was an accident."

"It's okay, he's fine, don't worry, it happens. I've stood on all of mine," I joked, and then remembering it, I winced at the memory of one of those times, when I accidentally kicked my Lace in the ribs as she came out of an agility tunnel and hit my running leg after I had commanded her wrongly. I had tried to avoid running into her at the same time as she tried to avoid me and in an effort to jump over her, had only succeeded in making the impact worse. She went flying and squealed in pain. To her it must have looked like I was making a kung fu kick at her. She was a very sensitive dog and it took many months for her to trust me so that we could do agility again.

The owner must have seen my anguish at the memory, and relieved that she was not the only one to feel sad about hurting their dog, she smiled at me briefly, said "Thank you" and then turned her attention back to Patch and continued to teach the task she had been given.

★

Over the next few weeks I saw her face change slowly but surely from angry, malevolent and unhappy to more relaxed, more accepting and even on occasion one of blatant happiness. At other times she descended back into sullenness and seemed still angry at Patch for existing. But Patch stayed consistent. He paid her attention every moment he was there and he worked hard to try to understand what she wanted of him. He was overjoyed each time she spoke to him, and he appeared totally immune to the malevolence that she still sometimes directed at him. He was friendly but uninterested in the other dogs or people; he only had eyes for her! It took some time, but during the course of the next few weeks she also started to dress more and more like a dog trainer, not an executive's PA. One day she even arrived with mud plastered all up her new trousers and over her new trainers.

Then things started to get even better: she started chatting with other owners in the class and she clapped and squealed with delight when one of the other class dogs learnt to put his head into a cone and keep it there. Such simple things began to delight her. *It was like she was coming back to life.* It was a joy to watch each week as she relaxed, smiled and got really involved in all things dog.

One day she stopped after class to talk to me and to thank me for my help. "I just never knew before that dogs had personalities. I thought all animals were – well – like nothing. I thought they were just dirty, smelly, hairy beasts. I didn't know they were intelligent, could think, and improve, and learn and even speak. I didn't realise how much fun it can be to teach them and watch them. This class and the dogs here have made me realise that I have been wrong. I didn't know that they could be so funny and clever, and so lovely to have around."

My heart was warming to her as her heart warmed to dogs and as she continued, "And my Patch!", she smiled as she looked down at him with a look of love. "He is so very funny. *I really love him!*"

She had been infected by the love of a dog. She was beginning to drown in amazement and love for an animal she had always hated and feared. She had previously thought them dirty, unhealthy and pointless. She had been bitten as a child and considered that they should all wear muzzles and be kept away from the public, locked in kennels where their smell and filth could be contained. But having watched her own dog and the dogs of others improve socially, have lots of fun, become more happy and relaxed and do some very clever and humorous things, she was beginning to be smitten.

★

As the course progressed, other dog owners in the class became increasingly drawn to Patch and laughed and smiled and clapped as they saw him demonstrate his obedience or his best trick. Patch's owner tried at times to hide it, but I saw her start to glow with pride at his and her every achievement.

Then, on the last night of the course, a hot, sultry evening, I went over to open a window as the dogs from Patch's class began to arrive. There in the car park stood Patch and his owner chatting to another owner and her dog. Patch was still looking up at her wagging his tail but she was increasingly engaged in the conversation. He pawed at her leg and she complied with his wishes and bent down briefly to stroke him.

That night, she sat near to the lady that she had been chatting with outside. I later learned that they had been out walking the dogs together several times. They continued to sit together and at times chat in class, and laughter and smiles flowed between them. Their dogs too got on really well and enjoyed each other's company. At the end of the night I asked everyone who was coming back to the next course to continue training, and Patch's owner spoke for both herself and her new friend: "We are!"

A friendship flourished and soon both ladies, each of them a widow for many years, had a new – and I suspect lifetime – friend.

As it turned out, Patch wasn't showing such great behaviour because he was in his honeymoon period, but instead it was just who Patch was. One of the most delightful and enchanting little dogs one could ever wish to meet, a dog who on many levels and in many ways really did 'do her some good'. Heck, he did everyone good, just watching him was fun; he was happy all of the time. It was infectious, irresistible and contagious. Some dogs really do have an air about them that infiltrates nearly everyone around them. Patch was delightful on every level and at times I wanted to pick him up and steal him so that he could infiltrate my house with his sheer joy of life.

★

As a dog owner and trainer I have come to realise that Patch's owner was not alone in her thinking about dogs being pointless, scary, smelly, dirty beasts. I have met many who have felt this way about dogs and other animals. It is sad for me to see people miss out on the joy that animals can bring. But as dog owners we must all consider that they probably have their reasons. Only in owning a well-behaved and well-mannered dog can we change their minds and help them discover the joy of dogs, and even then, only if they were 'meant to'.

It never ceases to amaze me just how big an impact a dog can have on a person or a family. Sometimes, sadly, that impact can be dreadfully bad: some people's lives are literally destroyed or upturned by a dog or puppy, which can be devastating for all involved. But most often I see new owners grow as humans, learn to care unconditionally, I see them acquiring new skills of communication and sociability as they talk to like-minded strangers who have dogs. I see people with mental or physical challenges thrive and shine when they have an outlet in their dog. I have seen sad people's hearts be healed, and new friendships get formed, because of their dogs. I've seen owners fall in love with a fellow owner, and I have watched people fall in love not just with their dog's cute fluff, but also with its *mind*, with its ability to make the most of things, their courage and their playfulness. I have seen people begin to shine when the 'dog penny' has dropped and they realise that no, we are not alone on this earth, for we have dogs and other animals too. All are as amazing as we are.

In knowing a dog, or any animal, something can come alive in us that was not alive before. For some people like me, sharing our life with an animal is essential for our wellbeing; for others it is a much-loved addition, but to others it is none of those things. None of these people are right or wrong; it doesn't make a person good or bad, wrong or right – just different.

But I know which one I prefer to be.

★

If you are still out there Patch, and have learnt to read, I'd like to say well done little fella; you mended an angry heart and healed a sad soul, brought many laughs to many people, and made two lonely ladies develop a strong and hopefully enduring friendship. You will always be remembered. Keep on wagging that tail, keep on having fun, and thank you for gracing all our lives with your wonderful disposition and personality.

My Lucky Day!

Throughout my life, and the lives of many that I know, there have been times when it would appear that some kind of power, force, or intervention takes place that defies my understanding, or their understanding. It appears that something or someone 'takes over' and makes stuff occur.

Some will call it God, or their version of God, or the Universe, the Higher Power, Fate, Destiny or the power of intention. Whatever one chooses to believe in. I have pondered such things deeply and have yet to conclude anything solid (I rarely conclude anything solid, I find that is the best way to keep an open mind). But I have concluded that there is definitely a force, a plan, guidance, or something that defies proper explanation but which on occasion just makes things happen.

★

I had decided that it was time I started to look for another dog. This time, a puppy. I wanted a male as I had two bitches and I had recently concluded that dog households appear to function better if there is a mix of both sexes.

Years before, I had met a red merle Collie, who was totally adorable, clever, brilliant, talented, gentle, stunning and adored. I also really liked and admired his owner. I fell instantly in love with him – I had never seen a red merle before and I was fascinated by his random-coloured coat. From that moment I knew that in my heart, at some point in my life, I wanted a red merle Collie.

But strangely, in my heart I also felt guilty for wanting to own the exact dog that I wanted to own. It is a curiosity of the human condition that some of us feel guilt for wanting what we want.

Despite the guilt, I followed my heart and I found a great breeder who sometimes produced red merles. We spoke at length on the phone; she quizzed me on the lifestyle I might offer a puppy. She accepted me as a potential puppy owner and I was put on the waiting list. I began the long wait that many of you will be familiar with for one particular bitch to come in season and then to be mated with one particular dog. Whilst I waited, I researched all I could about the potential parents' lines. And the more I looked, the more I liked what I saw. And so I waited. Whilst I continued to wait, I also looked for a few other breeders just in case the litter I was waiting for never happened.

I loved the next breeder I came across. Working line dogs, all bred for working ability and temperament. Looks, it seemed from this breeder's photo album, were simply not a matter of concern. There were long coats and short coats, prick ears and floppy, there were mostly black and white or black and white tricolours, but there were occasionally reds or red tris too. But his dogs look happy, well socialised, busy and physically fit! Just like the other breeder's.

The form I had to fill in to apply for a puppy from this breeder was extensive beyond compare. I liked that. Despite my 'credentials' I still wondered if I might not be accepted as a potential puppy owner. But I was. I was told that a mating was expected in about six months and to write back then.

The waiting for the first breeder's bitch to come in season continued. I knew the date that the season was due and I planned in my mind what date I would bring a puppy home. I was so excited but the waiting seemed endlessly frustrating. She never came in season on the expected date and the pain of waiting began to feel as if it might never end. Another six months came and went.

I was conscious that I had not written back to Breeder 2 and soon I started to feel guilty about that as well. So I continued the wait, and carried the guilt. In the end, I waited well over a year.

And then, one morning, it happened. It literally just happened. Just like that. I woke up and the very first thought I had was that *I can wait no more! I need a puppy now.* As I write this and look back on that day, I still cannot believe it happened. It seems an impossible story to believe, even for me and I was in it. But it did happen. I went to the kettle and made a drink. I took the mug of tea back upstairs to drink as I sat at my computer and booted it up. I composed myself for the honest email I was about to write to Breeder 2.

I apologised to Breeder 2 for not getting back in touch. I poured out my heart and explained about the guilty secret of wanting not just a healthy dog of good lines, but also, secretly, a red merle. I waffled on to him about how I had waited and waited for the first breeder's chosen bitch to come in season. I bumbled on honestly as best I could, about my innermost feelings about dogs and what they meant to me and all sorts of probably irrelevant stuff. Stuff he probably just glanced over and never thought of again.

And then, after I had poured out the truly irrelevant tirade of my entire heart and all my feelings and the deep longing I had had for a red merle... but acceptance that seemingly it 'wasn't meant to be' and a that a healthy black and white dog would suffice, I pressed the send button. Feeling suddenly tired, I went back to bed for a few minutes to daydream of my new puppy and hope that I might meet him soon. But within five minutes I heard my computer ping. I sprang out of bed and went to it in the hope that it was a reply to the message I had just sent.

And there it was; the life changing email reply from Breeder 2. It read:

Hi Denise, thank you for your message. This is weird. I don't know if this is fate or just your lucky day, but my daughter has a litter. They are eight weeks old TODAY. She has two red merle males available. She says that one of them is a very special boy, lovely markings too, and thinks he is perfect for you! This is her number, call her. I have already told her to expect your call. I hope you like him!

And then within an hour I was sent a picture of Connor. And my heart melted.

Within twelve hours we were driving up a long motorway to see him at his home.

He was beyond my wildest dreams. The whole litter looked well, happy and were wagging with friendliness and fun. But Connor, the pup his breeder had earmarked for me, kept coming to me more than the others. He was such a happy pup, friendly but gentle. He was so beautifully marked and had soft, kind eyes that I felt I could drown in. He was more than I had ever dared to dream of. And he was going to be mine.

After forty-eight hours, Connor was at home with us and he was set to become one of the most influential dogs I have ever known. He has gone on to be a great sheepdog, he has competed successfully in a few trials, he has won obedience competitions, he has done demos with me and he has been a gentle, calming influence on all my dogs and so much more as well.

★

Exactly what force led me to send that particular email on that particular day I will never know, but I do know that I am very grateful to it and that without it, I may never have known Connor and all that he brought to me.

And so my life with Connor and all that he has given me had begun.

May that force bless your life, as it has surely blessed mine.

Connor's Magic Oil

Sometimes something happens which, even though you witness it, you still cannot believe. Such is the story of the events surrounding Connor during 2018.

At the end of January 2018, Connor, who at the time was almost eleven years old, fell about twelve feet down into an abandoned lime kiln, landing on his rear end on a hard surface.

It was entirely my own fault that it happened and I will never forgive myself for it. A friend and I were walking the dogs in a place where my dogs and I had walked probably twice a week for Connor's whole life. The path was clearly marked and led its way between two deep holes, former lime kilns, which had recently been excavated and cleaned up. Further along the path was Connor's favourite swimming lake and as normal he was trotting peacefully towards it. He was mature and calm, and had never strayed off the path and so stupidly I had not put him on a lead. The other two dogs, much more lively and unpredictable than Connor, were on leads for their own safety. But I knew I could trust Connor to stay on the path, as I knew he would be committed to the straight route to his favourite lake. Oh, how I wish I had leashed him that day! *Or do I?*

I don't know why he did it, but he must have felt really happy and well that day, because he suddenly did this little hop, skip and a jump for joy and then threw himself at the ground for a roll of happiness, and as he rolled over, his back legs went over the edge of the vertical drop and his weight dragged his body over the edge. With the rest of his body dangling perilously into the hole, for a moment he clung to the edge with his front paws. His handsome face peered at me with a paw each side of it. I will never forget that moment. He had no idea the danger he was in and he looked kind of embarrassed, but pleading at me.

"Please help me, Mum," his eyes said. Horrified at the sight and knowing the danger he was in, I sprinted the few metres or so toward him.

I looked into his eyes and told him to "Hold on, Connor," but as I neared him, he lost his grip and he just slipped away and was gone from sight. As the sides of the hole had been recently cleaned and there was nothing to impede the fall, he went straight down vertically. Sickeningly, I heard the dull thud as he hit the ground many feet below.

With my heart in my mouth I peered tentatively over the edge. He was lying still on the ground in an uncomfortable-looking heap. *Oh my God, he is dead,* I thought, and my gut wrenched in pain at the sight, which I had caused through my own stupidity. Passing the leads of my other dogs to my friend so she could keep them safe I ran along the path, around the edge of another kiln and down the steep bank to the flat land below. As I ran toward him he started to move slowly and tried to get up.

Thinking his back might be broken I shouted, "Stay there, Connor." He struggled to his feet and then I was at his side. He just stood there, his head hanging. His eyes looked shocked and confused and his left hind leg was dangling limply. He swayed unsteadily on his right hind leg and I held him still as he gathered himself.

We were half a mile away from the car and I had no idea how I was going to get him back there. There was no vehicle access to this place, unless you had a quad bike, which I didn't. He was heavy, and lifting him would mean risking my damaged back, which at the time was in a dire state. If my back went, then I would be no use to him at all.

But realising that my only option was to carry the twenty-six kilogram dog back to the car, I bent down to lift him. Connor hates being lifted and he anticipated my move and stepped away from me, placing his injured leg tentatively on the ground. I was amazed! He could use the leg that had been hanging limply! He was very lame and clearly in shock but it seemed he could use the injured leg. *Perhaps he has been lucky and was just bruised*, I thought. As I looked up to the edge he had just fallen from I wondered how he could move at all, let alone walk! And so, with little other choice available to us, we began the long, limping walk back to the car. Adrenaline is a wonderful thing and it flowed with abundance through both Connor and I. It seemed it kept him going through the pain, and me through the worry. When we got to the car I succeeded in lifting him into it but he snarled and snapped at me as I did so, the pain now making him as aggressive as I had ever seen him, and I began to realise just how much pain he must be in. Adrenaline had got him to the car, but now the pain was overwhelming him.

He had X-rays at my own vet and was then referred to a specialist for a CT scan and a full MRI scan. These revealed that the fall had caused some bone fragments to fracture off his left hip, his spine and his pelvis. They also revealed pre-existing conditions: he had dysplasia in his left hip, the one that had just been further damaged, and extensive spondylitis of his lower back (a degenerative disease of the spine). As the surgeon talked me through the MRI scan he explained that the spondylitis had already been causing constriction around his spine where his sciatic nerve exited. The swelling produced from the fall had further compounded this and his sciatic nerve was now being crushed by it. There was extensive bruising and swelling in the area of his spine above the damaged hip joint. The surgeon's hope was that the bony fragments would settle where they were but he remained concerned about the extent of the bony growth caused by the spondylitis, which was beginning to impede his sciatic nerve.

"He may need spinal surgery if this worsens," he said solemnly, and my heart sank. "Furthermore," he said, "the crushing injury sustained in the fall may have destabilised his whole condition and his existing problems may worsen. He has had a very lucky escape, but may not be out of the woods yet." Poor Connor. What had I done? How could I have been so very stupid? I cursed and began to hate myself.

★

Prior to the accident, Connor had been reasonably fit for an older dog. Although at times he had shown stiffness in his hip and lower spine, as well as intermittent lameness in his front wrist and paws due to arthritis, he was still walking or swimming for two hours a day, every day. Connor has led a very active life. He did agility from the age of around eighteen months for around a year (until I become too lame) and then he began years of sheepdog training, real sheep work on the farm, and the occasional sheepdog trial. He had also trained for and competed successfully in a few obedience competitions as well as being one of my main demo dogs for public events and performances. He had had a lifetime of long-distance walking, hill and mountain walking and retrieving a ball, so his body was well worn. He had been treated for stiffness and pain at times over the preceding few years with Metacam when symptoms were evident, and a few weeks prior to the accident my vet had started him on twice-weekly laser treatment for his spine, hips, hocks, elbows, paws and wrists, where he had shown some signs of pain and occasional lameness. He had stopped routinely jumping in the car about a year prior to the accident and from that point I had been lifting his back end in for him, if he had not wanted to jump in.

As we studied the MRI scan, the surgeon advised that if all of those 'back end' problems were further destabilised by the fall, then from this point on Connor might go into decline. He recommended he begin treadmill hydrotherapy as soon as possible and he agreed that my own vet had already prescribed the best drugs for him: Tramadol for the pain, Gabapentin for the nerve pain, both three times daily, and Metacam for the pain and inflammation. His laser treatment was set to continue to promote healing and he was assessed for suitability for hydrotherapy every week.

For the first week, Connor lay on his bed and didn't really move much at all. I slept downstairs with him, took time off work, and stayed with him day and night. But he didn't really do anything. With my husband, Simon working hundreds of miles away from home, my friend Sophie Fisher and her dog-walking team from Max Dogs, to whom I will always be grateful, stepped in from day one and took the other dogs out walking for me while I stayed in with Connor. Bless him, every day, once a day for that first week, he struggled on three legs to go into the garden to toilet. He wouldn't let me help him and if Simon or I went near him he growled, such was his pain.

But apart from his daily toilet trip he really didn't move much at all. Trying to keep him entertained, as he lay on his bed, I rolled a ball to him and he caught it in his mouth and rolled it back, but for the first seven days or so that is all the activity he had. After seven days he started to come round a bit and he went into the garden a few more times a day but only to sniff, toilet and look around briefly before returning to his bed. At this stage I began to film him and share his progress with concerned friends on Facebook. On day eight he ventured out of the front door and across the road to the village green where he sniffed, toileted and returned.

Slowly he started to improve a little and I took him out more, to keep his mind and the good parts of his body active. Simon and I put him in the cage, lifted the cage into the car, and took him out down the local trail where the surface was flat and stable. During the week when Simon was working away, a good friend and neighbour, Louise, helped me with lifting his cage into the car for his walks and vet trips. By the end of week two he was showing definite signs of improvement, occasionally balancing on the injured leg to wee, and he even had a tentative scrape at the ground with the injured leg afterwards.

But whenever he tried to use the leg he quickly lifted it up high and it began to twitch, which we assumed was the trapped nerve. One day I took him out in the car to one of his favourite walks high up on a hill to cheer him up a bit as he seemed to be slipping into depression. He was so excited when he realised where he was going that when I opened the boot of the car, he did something he had never done before: he leapt out of the car without being given his release command. He ran a few yards on three legs before I yelled at him to stop, and when encountering a few rocks that had fallen from a wall, he tried to jump them, pushing himself off with his only good back leg. I'm not sure if he banged his trailing left hind leg as he did so, but that night his left hind foot started to swell.

As well as his veterinary meds, I had now started Connor with Reiki sessions, and he was also being given distance healing from a very kind and generous soul in the US, Alecia Evans, who had been monitoring his progress on Facebook.

For a while he mostly appeared to improve, but the improvements were short lived and by around week five he had started to visibly deteriorate again. He was looking more and more 'stoned' on his drugs. His eyes were blurry and he appeared to be losing interest in going out, spending more, not less, time on his bed. He began asking to go into the garden to eat grass and then be sick. This went on for several days, with the frequency of sickness increasing, and his interest in going out or doing anything other than eat grass was beginning to wane.

For no apparent reason he was getting worse, he was getting depressed, and every week he went for hydrotherapy assessment and every week he failed it.

Right from day one, seven different people had been contacting me and encouraging me to try him on CBD oil. CBD is an extract of the hemp plant (also known as cannabis sativa L). It is the non-psychoactive part of the plant, and as such its use is legal in the UK for humans and in many, but not all, countries worldwide, at the time of writing (January 2019). THC, which is the psychoactive part of the same plant, is illegal for general use in the UK and most other countries although it is widely used in medical and even veterinary care, and particularly with cancer patients, in some parts of the world.

Each of these people told a tale of what seemed like a miracle recovery for them or their animals on CBD. One of them, a friend who had been watching Connor's videos on Facebook, was an A&E nurse with over twenty years' experience. She had been badgering me from day one and telling me over and over that I needed to try this. She told me a hard-to-believe personal tale of her own 'miracle recovery' on CBD oil. She was a woman I both knew and respected, having met her when she attended one of my Turn and Face events a year earlier and witnessing her medical skills when she gave my Simon first aid after he accidentally cracked his head on something hard. I liked her, I trusted her experience, and I wanted to believe her.

I have always been open to alternative treatments and so I looked into CBD oil. So many of the stories I read seemed almost miraculous. People who had been struck down and even who were bedridden were taking this oil and then getting up, sometimes as little as a few hours later, and getting back on with life. Where pharmaceuticals had not helped, CBD was helping. But the stories seemed too good to be true. And what's more, while some people reported near miracles, others reported no benefit.

I asked my vet about trying CBD on Connor. She told me that she couldn't offer advice with regard to CBD and she certainly could not recommend that I give it to him in conjunction with his current medication regime.

After a night of going in and out of the garden almost continuously whilst Connor was being sick, I was worried that the meds were making him ill. He was getting more and more lethargic and non-responsive at times. I decided that I could no longer ignore the many people shouting at me to try CBD, and I made the decision to give it a go.

It was the Monday of week five of his recovery and I had another assessment for hydrotherapy that day, so remembering my vet's words about not trying CBD in conjunction with his vet meds, I decided I would stop them and give the recommended brand of CBD oil a go instead. Not knowing what CBD oil would do to Connor, I gave it to him immediately prior to leaving for the vets – a thirty-minute journey. I figured that if it was going to make him ill, then the best place for him to be ill was when he was already at the vet's.

I tried the oil myself and it tasted horrid. Knowing Connor was reluctant to take anything 'suspicious', I rolled up a ball of smelly gorgonzola cheese and put the recommended four drops inside and gave it to him. I crossed my fingers, loaded him into the car and took him for his fourth hydrotherapy assessment at the vet's. By now, I had trained him to go up and down a ramp to get into and out of the car. As I helped him down the ramp outside the vet's I observed that he looked exactly the same as he had thirty minutes earlier. He also looked worse than yesterday – probably because I had stopped his vet meds, I thought! Head hanging down low, he was hopping all the way and not using the leg at all. The hydro nurse and a passing vet in reception took one look at him and shook their heads sadly. I noted that the nurse also looked rather worried.

"Sorry Denise, but he still isn't fit enough. In fact, he doesn't even look as well as he did last week. I think maybe we need to have another look at him and see if something has been missed."

I felt the tears well up inside. They had confirmed what I had thought: he was getting worse, not better. The swelling on his foot was growing and he was getting depressed, and the CBD oil had made no difference at all. I helped him back up the ramp and took a slow drive home stemming the tears and the worry as I drove, wondering what on earth was going to happen next and whether Connor was going to need surgery after all. My heart was as low as it had ever been.

When we pulled up outside our home, Connor, unusually, stood up and started to bark. He had seen a neighbour who he liked and who only yesterday had been to visit him as Connor lay on his bed. He was wagging his tail and barking his hello through the window. As I attached the ramp to the back of the car and opened the boot, Connor pushed me away to get down it, and tail wagging, still barking hello at the friendly neighbour, *he proceeded to walk down the ramp and then he walked up the street using all four legs,* wagging and barking all the way as he went. He looked really happy. I could not believe what I was seeing! I know that my mouth was ajar as I stared at Connor in utter disbelief. It was a moment frozen in time and which I will always remember.

The neighbour, having seen us arrive in the car, stopped to ask how he was today, having seen him flat out and unmoving on his bed the evening before. His mouth fell open, mimicking my own, as Connor walked with only a small limp toward him. Neither of us could believe what we were seeing. I just stood and stared in disbelief. He was walking again and he looked like a completely different dog.

"Wow! He looks much better!" my friendly neighbour said as a smile spread right across his face. "That's such a difference from last night!" My face must have been beaming and I didn't know what to say. I didn't understand what I was seeing. It had been so long since I had seen that leg on the ground I was stunned and elated all at once. Connor seemed to have just come back to life: his head was held higher than it had been for weeks, he was using his leg at every stride, and his limp was hardly evident.

It had been precisely one hour and fifteen minutes since I had given him four drops of CBD oil and he looked almost like a dog with no injury. All those stories I had read and disbelieved about miracle cures, and now I was witnessing one. After greeting the neighbour and making a big happy fuss of him, Connor then proceeded using all four legs to walk back to our home and up the thirteen steps to our front door, using his bad leg every stride. Then he went out into the garden and did a huge wee and scraped his bad leg on the ground, before having a shake and then hurling himself at the ground for a joyous roll. He was like a completely different dog. I was totally stunned by this very surreal event.

Back indoors, I rang Simon. He sounded doubtful, as if he didn't believe me, so later that night I sent him a video of Connor playing with his ball in the living room, fetching it and bringing it back, using his leg at every stride.

That same evening, the swelling on Connor's affected foot disappeared completely, never to return.

I rang the vet's and told them that Connor had just started to walk again. It was less than two hours since I had left the surgery, so their voices sounded very sceptical. I said I wanted to take him in the following morning for another hydro assessment and for them to witness the dramatic change that had occurred.

As he walked down the ramp on all four legs and into the vet's waiting room the following morning, there were many medically wise faces peering at him. Only yesterday they had thought he was deteriorating, but today he was walking almost without a limp. He was booked in for hydrotherapy at once and started attending weekly sessions. Everyone was thrilled if utterly bemused by this sudden turn of events and so it was that I admitted to the CBD 'crime' I had committed. They were baffled, but thrilled for Connor and for me.

The next day Connor started to trot out on his daily walk. I tried to slow him down as I felt it was all going too fast but he had other ideas. After four days on CBD, when he walked it was impossible to see that there was anything wrong with Connor at all. He was trotting really well, although he still had a slight limp in trot. Two weeks later he was running in the snow and throwing himself in it to roll. Every day I extended his walks, until soon he was again walking for an hour twice a day. My wise vet advised me to stop him from cantering for a few more weeks, but Connor was getting so much better each day that he had started to run about in the garden, the house and on the green. He started to jump for joy again and roll around in the grass and be a normal dog. The 'stoned' look had gone, and every day, strength and life returned to him.

The whole story was recorded on video and uploaded onto Facebook, and Connor's recovery attracted worldwide attention. CBD oil user groups started to ask to use the videos for marketing and promotion purposes and people started to flood my inbox with enquiries of what Connor was on and where could they get it. I took Karma off the Metacam she had been having for hip pain and put her on CBD too, with the same success. Simon and I started to have it for our daily back pain, also with great results. Now, all three dogs and two humans in our household were having it.

At the time of writing, neither Connor nor Karma have had any drugs for pain or inflammation since their first day on CBD (apart from one single tablet as a trial – see later in this chapter). Simon has reduced his daily pain meds significantly, and at times CBD has been his only pain relief. I no longer have pain meds for my back pain at all; I just take CBD.

A few weeks went by and all was going well, until one day I dashed out in the morning and forgot to give us all our 'magic oil'. Connor was immediately struggling again. He was lethargic and plodding and didn't want to trot. We met up with friends and they asked why he was so low that day, and I explained I had forgotten his oil. I videoed the event and uploaded it on Facebook. I gave him some oil as soon as I got home and then in the afternoon I videoed him again and uploaded that, for everyone to see. The results were truly astonishing: in the morning, without his oil, he was plodding, stiff and miserable. In the afternoon he was running, bounding and barking with joy. The videos spread far and questions came in as to what brand of oil he was on. I then started to stock the oil for my clients and friends and increasingly strangers who came my way to ask about 'Connor's magic oil'.

Connor went from strength to strength and more and more people asked me to supply them with CBD. It soon became clear that for some people and dogs, CBD oil had the same seemingly miraculous effects, but for others it had little or no effect. It became apparent also that whilst some open-minded people were keen to try this on their young injured dogs, others were deeply wary of it and open to it only when they had failed with everything else and as a last resort, often when their dog was close to dying. Sadly, for dogs who were ill due to old age it had much less effect. CBD doesn't seem to cure old age symptoms, or prevent death. But for some, it worked as well for their animals or themselves as it had for Connor.

Connor continued to improve at lightning speed. Vets, nurses and all our friends started to become fascinated with the very dramatic and rapid progress he was making. Friends who had seen Connor before the accident and then saw him after CBD oil all commented that he seemed happier, friendlier and more alert and lively than he was *before* the accident. I have now looked at photographic evidence and it is true that Connor's head and ear carriage after going on CBD oil is higher and more alert than before he had the accident. He is happier in himself. He is more active and he has become lively in the evenings, whereas a year or so earlier he had started to become lethargic. Whatever it is doing to him, he is *better* than he was during the months and years preceding the accident. Who could ever have imagined that Connor having such a terrible fall and suffering such horrible injuries would have led to him ending up *better off than he was before the accident?* Many other people and their dogs who had tried CBD as a result of seeing Connor's recovery videos were also better off.

So. *Do I wish I had kept him on a lead that day and prevented the accident, or not? I just don't know. I wish he had never had to suffer, for sure. But he is so much better off now as a result of CBD that it is hard to say.*

It took a few more weeks in total for Connor to fully extend the injured leg that he had carried for five weeks and regain the capacity to run flat out after a ball. But soon the videos I posted showed a Connor who was looking like he had no injuries at all, even though presumably the left-hip dysplasia problem and the spondylitis continued to deteriorate with increasing age.

Later in the year I tried several times to wean Connor off his oil, just to see if it was actually still doing anything. Each time we had the same results: he was fine for a day or two but then he showed signs of real stiffness and he started to get miserable again. So back on the oil he went, and each time he improved immediately.

But my journey into the world of CBD oil wasn't over yet. In November 2018 I had another great learning experience with it. One of my friends who had used my CBD oil on his dog had then tried a different brand. It claimed to be exactly the same constituents and strength, but it was a *lot* cheaper. I had been told many times that you often 'get what you pay for' with CBD, with some brands known to be less useful than others. But as I was now selling the CannaWell brand, I thought it only fair to people who had decided to buy from me that I test this for myself. I needed to see if all oils are the same; whether I could get the same results with this cheaper oil. Again I recorded the results and shared the daily videos on Facebook for all to see.

After one day, all three dogs were still well. On the second day, too. On day three I was not sure that Connor looked so well in the morning and by the early afternoon I was totally convinced that he was not at all well. He was reluctant to walk, stiff and short of stride and he would not trot. But most noticeably, on day three, all three dogs had a dramatic shift of behaviour that I was not expecting. They began to sniff the ground, seemingly looking for something. When they found that something, they ate it! All three began to pick up bits of gravel from the floor and crunch it, Karma started to lick trees and at home the wall, Connor licked the floor and started to dig small holes in soil, and try to eat something in there, and Cherry licked the floor and mud. They were sniffing in a way I had never seen them do before, and this, added to the fact that Connor was definitely very uncomfortable made me abandon the trial that same afternoon and take them home to give them CannaWell once again. Within two hours they were back to normal, though they seemed sleepy.

However, the following day there was again a dramatic shift from normal behaviour. I got up and took them out first thing in the morning as per usual, having given them all their oil. The walk went by without incident, Connor was back to walking, trotting and running as normal and all three had ceased the sniffing and licking and eating of 'things'. Unusually, when I arrived home after the walk, instead of hovering around waiting for breakfast as they normally do, they all went straight to bed and slept solidly all day, until I woke them for their afternoon walk. I was bemused. Again, in the afternoon they all walked as usual and seemed normal, but once more on returning home they just went straight to bed and straight to sleep. I had never known them do this before and it reminded me of how a dog behaves when it is in recovery from illness or accident. *But recovery from what?* I wondered.

I started to talk to lots of people with experience of CBD who suggested that they had perhaps picked up some contaminant from the 'trial' oil. CannaWell were just about to announce that they had been certified organic – something I knew they had been trying to achieve for over a year, throughout the time I had been using their product. None of the other companies that I had looked at were organic. The oil I had trialled was not organic; meaning that the plants they were taking oil from *may have had* fertilisers, pesticides or other contaminants on them or in them. CannaWell, being organic, did not.

I spoke to a vet and she advised that licking walls and floors can be a sign of liver failure. I was horrified. Had it been the case that I had given my dogs a trial CBD which contained contaminants that had caused their livers to struggle? If this was the case, then that would explain why the dogs had been so sleepy the night after the trial ended and the following day: they *were* in recovery.

Of course I can never know for sure what had happened to cause their odd behaviour but it was enough for me to think that I would *only ever* give my dogs CBD oil that was organic and certified as pesticide and fertiliser free. Of course it would be more expensive than non-organic oils, because crop yields would be potentially much lower, but it was certainly safer, in my view.

★

As I finish writing this chapter of the book it is February 2019, just over a year since Connor's accident. Connor is drawing close to his twelfth birthday. Whilst Connor remains much happier, brighter and more alert than he was before he went onto CBD oil, sadly he has not been totally problem free. In recent months he has shown further signs of intermittent lameness in his front feet. After a break of a few months he is now back on weekly laser treatment for this lameness. Additionally, he is finding it harder and harder to sit – the action is stiff and slow where years ago it was fast and fluid. He still cannot get by without his 'magic oil' and since the arrival of winter I have increased his dose to five drops, twice daily, which seems to have helped. This is still a relatively low dose so there is room for further increase if necessary. A few months back he also started to show signs that he may have a trapped nerve in his spine, as the surgeon suggested might happen. This only shows itself when I lift his back end into the car, so we have ceased that activity and now only allow him car access via the ramp, which has alleviated the problems.

Throughout January 2019, Connor didn't seem his normal self. He seemed a little down and on six occasions he refused to go for his afternoon walk. I went to the vet's and had full blood tests done and a thorough check-over. Although his blood results were very good, sadly he was found to have a grade three heart murmur as well as pain in his lower spine. For one day and one day only, I tried him on the drug Gabapentin again to see if it would help with the pain. Immediately he began to look 'stoned' again, he wobbled as he stood, and he held his head low. Clearly this medication didn't help him so after just one tablet, I ceased it.

Connor has now had a heart scan and the problem has been diagnosed as a leaky valve, probably caused simply by age, and a slightly enlarged heart which has grown to counteract the leaky valve. At this stage it is thought that medication is not necessary and he is due back for a heart scan six months after the first one.

At the end of January, Connor began to return to normal. I am unwilling to put him through scans again at this stage so

I can only hope that the problems he had that month were just an arthritic flare-up or some exercise-related injury. But for now at least the minor crisis seems to have passed. He is getting no younger; perhaps old age is just catching up on him?

I don't know what the future holds for Connor as he ages further and his busy, active life continues to take its toll. I hope with all my heart that he never arrives at the point where he needs surgery on his spine. But old age is old age and there is nothing that can be done about it. So all I can do is hope and pray that the beautiful, gentle soul that he is has a good journey into his later years and that CBD continues to help him as he ages and the changes within him continue to progress.

★

I would like to make clear that in no way am I anti veterinary medicines, or human medicines for that matter. I have seen amazing things happen due to pharmaceutical drugs and I will no doubt use them for me and my dogs in the future. But I have had experiences in the past (particularly with my Cloud who had many bone problems and was on long-term pain medications that ultimately caused her to have a stomach ulcer, followed by other problems that ultimately caused her demise), which suggest that long-term use of some of these medicines can have a very detrimental effect. My experiences this last year with CBD have made me think that if an animal or human can get by on a natural product such as this which appears to have so few side effects and provides amazing results, then this should be more widely known than it is. Yes, CBD is a product of the cannabis plant. For many this in itself holds fear, but for me it has proven its worth and it has made Connor's life better and it has meant that all five of us, people and dogs in this household at least, are less reliant on the more commonly used pharmaceuticals.

I only wish I had known about CBD before, so that I could have tried it for poor Cloud. I wonder if her untimely and sudden end might have been different had I known about CBD back then?

I am not an expert on CBD or pharmaceutical drugs. But I hope that I have offered here an insight into something that may be of interest to others and a story of hope that even where some licensed drugs might fail, there *may* be a suitable natural alternative that really does work!

At time of writing, CBD oil is sold as a food supplement for humans in the UK and most of the world and as such can be manufactured and sold by virtually anyone. It is an unregulated industry and as such it is difficult to establish the quality of such products. Late in 2018 the UK Veterinary Medical Directorate wrote to sellers of CBD oil and stated that CBD can no longer be labelled and sold for pet use, as it had, get this, "been recognised as an effective medicine for animals". Meaning that they no longer classed it as a food supplement but as a medicine for animals and therefore it needs to be sold under a veterinary licence. Effectively this means that whilst humans can just buy it and use it, you now need to seek a prescription from your vet to give your animals CBD. The product, Hemp Balance, which is made by a company called CannaWell, is the one I have used for Connor since day one, and is created for humans, not animals. I made a personal choice to give it to my dog.

I would like to make clear that I am NOT being sponsored to promote this or any other product or service within this book. I am sharing this because I feel it information worth knowing. Not in an effort to seek sponsorship or financial gain.

★

I would like to thank the brilliant Emma and all of the extraordinary vets, nurses and team at STAR veterinary practice for providing not just outstanding, top-rate veterinary care to Connor, but also for providing me with emotional support and cups of tea as I awaited news of Connor's fate. Thank you also for not shouting at me for trying CBD.

I would like to thank Catherine of CannaWell for providing such an amazing product that brought my gorgeous boy back to life, for all your help, knowledge, support and a first-rate customer service.

I'd like to thank Tina Bowen for pointing me in the direction of CannaWell and in so doing, changing Connor's and my life so much for the better, as well as all the other friends and contacts who pushed me to try CBD in the first place.

I'd like to thank Sophie Fisher and the team at Max Dogs for taking care of the other dogs whilst I stayed home and cared for Connor. First-rate service and happy, tired dogs to boot.

I'd like to thank Alecia Evans and the lovely Reiki lady Rachel for your time and kindness in helping Connor with your little bit of 'healing magic'.

And I'd like to thank Sharon Nelson for your wisdom, experience and information about organic CBD (Sharon produces organic Manuka honey with CBD in it) in the US.

It has been a time of great learning for me, and of great benefit to Connor and the others in this house. I hope that this story may bring help and hope to others and their animals.

May the great green plant bring pain-free days to you all.

Mowgli

When I went into dog training, I had hoped that I would spend my days improving the lives of people and dogs. I wanted to bring hope to the owners of challenging dogs, understanding where there was none, and light to the end of tunnels. And in many ways, and on most days, that is exactly what has happened. But very sadly, every day is not like that. When working with dogs and people you also get to see some problems that cannot be cured, some situations that cannot easily be resolved, and on the worst days of all you face danger, fear and heartbreak. This story is about one of those days.

★

When the call came in it was clear from the very start that this was going to be a tough case.

The owner's voice indicated that something was very amiss. She sounded wary, cautious, frightened, and reluctant to share in some ways, but also desperate. I listened with growing concern as she gave me the details of the problem she had with her dog.

Mowgli had recently found himself a new home with two adoring and committed owners. He had been in rescue just a few short weeks, having been found tied to a tree with no history available, before these two kind souls, his new owners, had given him a home of love and one which they had promised him in their hearts would be his forever home.

Just a week after he had arrived at his new home his lady owner had fallen and broken her leg badly, and was having daily care-workers to help her get by. Shortly after her injury and whilst she was still very wobbly on her crutches, Mowgli, a huge dog, had apparently knocked her down and jumped on her, grasping her shoulder in his giant mouth, causing extensive bruising and also blood loss.

This did not sound good at all! All of a sudden, I felt a headache coming on.

His owner reported tearfully that although she loved the dog dearly she was now frightened of him, and asked me to see them as soon as I could.

I shuffled some appointments around, and asking my colleague Kate to attend with me, I made an appointment to visit their home the very next day. I was not looking forward to this visit one bit, but I hoped that when I saw him I would be able to understand more and be able to help in some way.

The day dawned and we were on our way. I noted that I had a very heavy heart and a feeling of doom as I drove the thirty miles to their home. We parked nearby and walked toward their house, which I noted with concern had a front door which was directly on the roadside pavement. There was no garden at all; the door was the only barrier between the pavement and their entrance hall. As we entered the house, Mowgli kept his distance and eyed us without a discernable expression from the kitchen where he had been put, behind a child gate, whilst we entered.

He was *huge*. She had told me on the phone that he was thought to be a Rottie X. Looking at him, I would say he was perhaps a Rottie crossed with something bigger, maybe a Burmese Mountain Dog or similar. He was so gorgeous though that despite what I had been told about his unfriendly behaviour, I fell for him. He was all fluffy ears and had a beautiful rich coat of gold and black. I so hoped that I could help him and his now-nervous owners.

He was usually unperturbed by visitors, I was told, so as he appeared calm, his owner released him into the living room where Kate and I sat. And stupidly, I allowed it to happen.

Kate and I sat on an old sofa, side by side. The seat had had many years of use and it had collapsed somewhat, meaning that as we sat our knees were higher than our pelvises, an uncomfortable and somewhat limiting position.

Mowgli regarded us briefly from a distance before appearing to disregard us completely, and he turned to his male owner who immediately started to stroke him and talk lovingly to him. I was in awe of his sheer size and power and I watched in fascination as he moved with all the prowess of a fit Shire horse across the room. Powerful, huge and very handsome.

As the story unfolded I learnt that when Mowgli first arrived in the home he had been quiet, somewhat withdrawn, but occasionally affectionate. They had quickly become besotted with him. They had always wanted a giant breed and were delighted that they were able to offer this dog a new home, after the sad tale they had been told about him being tied to a tree and being found, wet, bedraggled and very hungry.

But soon after his arrival he had started to bark at the front door, which opened straight out onto the pavement outside. This is a domestic set-up that so very often causes issues for guarding breeds, who can come to view their home as being under continuous threat. Their back garden had a rather old and battered fence on one side, on the other side of which was a public footpath. The fence was not considered secure, so when he went out there, they had tied him on a long line to the washing line post to make sure he couldn't escape and get lost again. Plans were afoot to re-fence the garden in a few days' time so Mowgli wouldn't have to be tied up and could roam free. But in the last week, Mowgli had started to bark and lunge at the fence as people passed by, as he did at the front door.

The female owner told me how a few days previously, he had been barking a lot at people going by and as she had hopped rather unstably on her crutches into the hall, to quieten him and stop him from jumping at the door, he had turned on her, knocked her to the floor and then pounced on her, proceeding to maul her arm and shoulder. He had stood over her and shaken her arm several times. Her screams had alerted her husband, who had come running down the stairs and shouted at Mowgli. Mowgli had released her, and wandered off to the kitchen.

"Later," she continued, "he came over to me and licked me as I cried. I think he felt guilty." She looked at him lovingly but there was also great wariness in her eyes.

The bruising caused was still evident on her hand, so I asked if we could see the extent of her injury under her jumper. She removed her jumper to reveal bruising from her fingers, right up one arm and across the right side of her chest. There were canine tooth marks on her upper arm and on the soft flesh on the inside of her elbow, showing the enormous width of this huge dog's bite. I was shocked into silence by what I saw.

It never fails to amaze me that some owners who suffer severe bites from their dog are still in love with them. Some owners are terrified of their dog when I first meet them, but yet they still love them. It is positive testament to the human

MOWGLI

condition, I feel, that some are capable of such generosity of spirit. As she spoke of the incident, Mowgli went over to her, wagged his tail a little and asked for a head rub, which she proceeded to give him, albeit somewhat cautiously. She smiled at him with love. "I think he is sorry he did it," she said. She looked at me as if seeking my agreement with this hopeful, loving thinking that she continued to feel somewhere inside.

A period of time passed whilst I observed the interaction, and then suddenly the interaction stopped and Mowgli left his owner. He took one step towards Kate and me, then paused, as if making a decision, and then he slowly turned his back on us both and lay down in the middle of the floor as if we were not even there and were certainly of no importance to him. It is very unusual for a dog to turn its back on a visitor to its home if it is not familiar with the visitor. It was an act of confidence on his part. He was self-assured and felt no threat from us. I felt a growing discomfort. I had dreaded the case since the first phone call, but his utterly dismissive attitude towards the two strangers in his home made me feel even worse.

Then came an even bigger surprise: "You see, it's not the first time he has done it," she revealed. "The first week he was here, before I broke my leg, he jumped at me and grabbed my hand when I tried to stroke him when he was eating a chew, over there." She pointed at his giant bed on the floor. Her face fell as the memory hit her. "But we love him so much, can you help us?"

At that point what I should have done was ask for Mowgli to be removed from the room so that Kate and I could feel safer. So that we could all have been safer. But I didn't want to do that in case the owners were upset and I was yet to uncover a *perfectly valid reason* why Mowgli had performed the attacks. Though what could possibly constitute a 'valid reason' for such behaviour I did not and still do not know. I didn't want to upset them for no reason and I still wished to observe the dog. I should have listened to what my intuition was telling me, but I had grown complacent in my experience. Or lack of appropriate experience. I had never seen a dog attack a human without any reason in my work with dogs and I thought that that was how dogs were, back then. In the days before Mowgli. So I had thought that as long as Kate and I did nothing at all to arouse the dog in any way, that we would all be safe. The lesson I learned that day is important for all of us.

As the consult proceeded, I learnt that Mowgli was becoming increasingly reactive toward passers-by in the street and in the garden. His barking was getting worse and he seemed more and more aggressive. "But he is just protecting his home, I guess?" With hope in his voice, the male owner had interjected.

Dogs that live in houses whose front door goes straight onto the pavement where people pass by often develop heightened levels of alertness, and reactivity. In these situations, from the dog's point of view, the door, the edge of their territory, is almost continuously under threat. Each passer-by represents a potential 'security breach', particularly if the dog's breed leans toward a guarding attitude. When they bark, the person goes away, much like the postman does, and this bolsters their confidence and belief that they need to bark to make them go away. Interestingly, some dogs don't bother protecting their home in this way at all, if they have no genetic or learnt predisposition to guarding, but instead they may be excited at the prospect of people coming near and maybe into their home. But those with guarding genetics can begin to spend their days in hyper vigilant mode, ready to take action each time anyone walks down their street. In Mowgli's case this was heightened even further by the public access that bordered one side of the garden, meaning that whether he was in the house or in the garden, his territory was continuously under threat. He was always vigilant and as each day went by frustration emerged, because although to the dog their barking appears to ward off the immediate threat, it doesn't stop new threats (new people) from coming their way. As their efforts fail to prevent new threats (more people coming past) so often they escalate their efforts and their behaviour worsens.

Interestingly, and often, some such dogs can also have a tendency to develop on-leash reactivity or aggression when out walking. Their territory starts to extend from the house to the pavement outside, to the street they live on, to their village or town, as they seek to ward off the threat to them, their home, or their owners, earlier – at the end of the road, further on in the village. It is common in cases of leash reactivity that the problem begins in the home and works its way out further and further from the house over time. Often these dogs do not display on-leash reactivity if they are taken on holiday or to a strange place, but continue to react in their local area. It is one of the most common causes of leash reactivity and I see such cases often.

Whenever I do a consult with a person about their dog, I always bear in mind that what they wish to achieve is the key component to success or not. If they have realistic expectations and are flexible in their approach, then most often huge strides can be made and the likelihood of a successful outcome rises. What they 'want' is after all what I am there to achieve. It is not about what I want, or what the internet says they should want, or what their peers tell them it should be. It is about what *they* want.

So having taken as much history as was available about this dog with no known background and having seen the evidence on her arm, I asked the ever-important question I so often ask, which reveals their inner desire.

"So. If I had a magic wand and could wave it and do anything you wanted, what would you have me do?"

There was a pause as the owners looked at each other. Then they looked at Mowgli, then back at each other before the lady of the house turned to me, biting her lip to stem some emotion, and spoke her heart's desire.

"I would like for you to make sure he never, ever, does anything like this again. I'd like for you to make him safe and make me feel safe." She looked down at the floor. I think something in her was telling her that this was an unrealistic expectation.

I paused in contemplation before considering my words carefully. My heart was very heavy indeed. The headache I had when I had taken the original phone call from them suddenly returned and I felt my heart booming in my chest. I wanted to help, but I felt uneasy, worried, frightened for them. I was about to deliver news that I knew was going to be unwelcome. I opened my mouth to speak, then shut it again as the gravity of my thoughts and the consequences of my words slammed me. They would be upset, and that is not what I wanted to be doing, so I allowed the words to come slowly to fruition.

As they waited, I began an internal wrestle with myself in an effort to find a way to avoid what I knew deep down I needed to say. I had no wish to cause them pain. They were lovely people doing a kind thing, giving a dog another chance. So I began to question myself in my mind. Maybe if they moved house, to where Mowgli's guarding response was not continuously ignited it might be okay? Maybe if we trained him to do something more productive rather than live on his nerves, guarding at every moment? Maybe something in his food had triggered this? Maybe he had a brain tumour, which was causing this behaviour? Maybe he had tremendous pain that caused him to be intolerant and overly reactive? The vet

The very talented Ace.

A perfect day for lovely Cooper.

Puppy Cloud. Right from day one it was clear that Cloud had 'attitude'.

She exuded such confidence for a seven week old pup out on her first walk.

If I tried to hold her, she bit me.

Cloud.
The most extraordinary
dog I have ever known.

Age brought out a more
ameniable side to her.

And finally she was
my best friend
and protector.

Poor Bruce, so poorly after the attack.

Bruce back in good health with his best mates, Karma,
Connor and Cherry. His attitude toward other dogs
remained completely unchanged by the attack.

My amazing Cassie. She had the brains and the speed to be great at Agility.

But my dog was about to recover my 'cool' for me.

Cassie and Lace, both great agility dogs.

My Beautiful Lace, a love monster in the extreme.

2018. Up to date, Denise and the gang; Cherry,
Conner and Karma

August 2018 – My mate Connor, back in great health.

A lovely, gentle pup, he turned into an excellent sheepdog.

And a great obedience dog too!

I remembered all the places we
had been to, the oceans we
had crossed together, the
sites we had seen…

I had only known him four years, surely this
couldn't be the end, could it?

had already checked him out and thought nothing was wrong, but he had not been able to examine him fully as the dog had been so unfriendly and volatile. Maybe if we had strict management in place when it came to feeding chews or things likely to invoke a guarding response? Maybe we could change the house so that he wasn't allowed near the front door? Maybe I had missed something? Maybe I was in the wrong job?

Doubt and concern spiralled around one another in my mind as all eyes rested on me waiting, waiting for my answer. If he had been smaller it would have been easier. But he wasn't. And the haunting doubt kept coming back; maybe I had missed something?

In many ways this case looked to be heading so obviously in one direction that I was kidding myself that I could ever make this dog safe, or make the lady feel safe. Would it even be wise or ethical to try? What if what I suggested failed and the dog killed her, or someone else?

Nah, I was kidding myself. I wanted it to be different, I so wanted it to be different, I wanted to bring good news, but this was not a safe dog.

I was silenced by my thoughts and my doubts as all the eyes looked on. I decided I wasn't good enough at this job and that they needed a second opinion. I would refer them to someone who knew more than me, someone older than me, someone perhaps more experienced with this breed type.

But maybe this would give false hope and that wasn't fair. I am pretty sure I knew what he would say anyway, and it wasn't fair to pass on a case and the associated expense and time and fruitless hope. But I just didn't want to deliver such awful news.

But as I wrestled with my doubts silently, Mowgli made the decision for me when he did something that I had never, ever, seen any dog do before. Mowgli got up from lying down and without looking at anyone, left the room and headed for the kitchen. He plodded slowly and methodically away from us all. We all watched him go. Then came the sound of slow lapping as he drank from his water bowl. Then the sound ceased and there was a slight pause before the big dog re-entered the living room. From the moment he came back we observed a change in him. The atmosphere in the room changed also and it seemed that Mowgli had made some decision or other.

Kate and I shifted uncomfortably on the sofa. As he came around the corner and into view, his eyes connected with Kate's, and slowly, with confidence and commitment, he strode directly at her with fixed intent in his eyes. His eyes were still locked onto hers as I heard her take in a deep gasp. *What on earth was he planning to do? I began to panic inside.* Time began to slow. I'd only ever seen a dog do this once before, when two much smaller Border Collies that were in my care had advanced with intent onto a stranger who had appeared in my garden one day. That day they had stalked the man as if he were prey. Mowgli was now preying on Kate, but Mowgli was much, much bigger than those Collies and Kate was sitting below his jaw line, slumped into the chair. Something which on reflection I now realise I should never have allowed to happen. Whatever Mowgli had in mind for Kate was my own stupid, naïve fault.

Slow deliberate pace followed slow deliberate pace as he continued across the room for what felt like hours, but must have been only a few seconds. His head was lowered and he glowered at poor Kate. He looked part lion, part wolf, his advance secure in confidence, menacing and unrelenting. The atmosphere in the room seemed to have changed and it felt oppressive, airless and stifled by fear.

I felt the adrenaline hit me as the threat to Kate loomed ever closer. I had to put a stop to this *now*, but how? If we moved it would be 'curtains' for one of us, I felt certain. Movement would be sure to ignite him further. They were a few seconds of my life that I will never forget: the fear, the uncertainty, the not knowing how to stop it.

As Kate and I sat on the collapsed sofa, Mowgli was above us in height; his lower jaw was probably level with Kate's cheekbone, and his head was considerably wider than hers. He continued his advance. He passed by both his owners as they stared on. For a moment I was totally frozen by his advance. Neither Kate nor I was breathing, locked in this moment of unknowing terror. Still he kept coming. Still we sat frozen. His intent seemed to actually immobilise us, like he was already controlling us. And still my mind offered no ideas as to how to rescue this situation.

I had heard people say 'I was frozen in terror' and now I knew what they meant. As if no matter what I did, fate was the only thing that would decide the outcome.

I must act now! Finally an idea formed and the words found an exit. "Please call his name!"

Mowgli was now just an inch or two from Kate's face and showed no signs of halting. I could smell his breath. She could probably feel it.

"What, now?" the man replied.

"YES, NOW!"

And thankfully, he did. "Mowgli, come here." He slapped his thigh to gain his attention. Mowgli stopped his forward movement and paused as Kate and I sat immobile. He continued to stare for a few seconds, deep into Kate's eyes, then he finally responded to his owner's words and turned and slowly walked away. On reaching his owner, he stood looking at him, with his back to us, as if we counted for nothing. I let out the breath that I had held and turned to Kate. She was ashen-faced and sweating. She looked like she had seen not one but a thousand ghosts, but at least she had started to breathe again.

The owners, even though they were not familiar with canine body language and behaviour were looking somewhat uneasy – they might not have read his intent, but they had felt the change of atmosphere as he had advanced on Kate, I am sure. They had not enjoyed witnessing this stalk either. Suddenly, my mind was made up. All my previous doubts were gone.

When struggling to find the right words to deliver in a difficult case, I always follow the same rule: be kind and be honest.

"I must pay homage to your efforts with Mowgli and your clear love of him, but I am afraid that in all my years working with dogs I have never encountered a dog that has knocked down and injured his owner before. I am sorry but I feel I am unable to help you to feel safe around Mowgli, nor prevent him from doing anything like that again." I pointed at her arm. "I am so sorry that I have to deliver this news. He is so cute and cuddly looking, but I don't think that Mowgli is really suitable as a pet dog. I could refer you to someone else, but I am pretty sure that they will agree with my views." I paused as the words sank in and watched as both their faces fell into sadness. "I am so very sorry," I concluded.

I just hate, hate, hate when I have to say words like these. Thankfully, it doesn't happen at all often, but every now and again it has to be said for what it is. In the same way that some cars and car drivers are not safe to be on the road, some dogs are not suitable as pets. And any dog who is willing to knock down and maul an already injured person is not a safe dog to have around any human, no matter what behaviour change work is done, in my opinion. "Can you put his lead on now please, whilst we talk?"

We chatted some more, but once the lead was on Mowgli turned and once more started to stare at Kate. Had he not had his lead on I felt sure his advance on her might have recommenced, so I asked them to put Mowgli in the kitchen and close the door so that Kate and I could breathe easily and feel safe once more.

Looking back on the case, in reality, I think that before we had even arrived at their home, in their hearts they had both realised that Mowgli was unsafe. But they didn't want to give up on him up without trying. Sometimes owners have a feeling that they don't like within them, but they need someone else to agree with them, so that they don't suffer the burden of such sad feelings and a difficult decision alone.

★

That night I contacted three very experienced trainers to ask their views on the case and on my decision. The one who I had considered referring him to stopped me mid-sentence as I started to explain. I hadn't said much before he had formed his final opinion. He said, "Denise, a large dog, with an unknown background, that has knocked down an already injured owner and caused the damage you describe is not safe to have in a domestic home. He probably isn't safe anywhere." Two other wise souls agreed. I felt relieved that I had them to confirm my decision, but it didn't make me any less sad about Mowgli or his owners. Tomorrow would be a horrid day.

I spoke at length with the owners on the phone the following day. It seems that overnight they had both arrived at the same conclusion as I had. There is no way they would ever trust him again, no matter what work was done. They loved him, and I could see in some ways why they did, he looked so cuddly and cute. But they knew deep down that the attack on the lady owner was one which they were unlikely to ever get over. They were heartbroken that they had to let him go.

Poor Kate will never forget the incident and I hold myself accountable for allowing it to happen. I am so very thankful that it ended with my friend and colleague still alive and well, but it taught me a good lesson. I had been too casual in my approach as I had never met a dog like Mowgli before. Since that case, dogs which have presented as serious biters are kept on-lead and away from me and anyone else that I may have with me, at least until we've had the chance to observe them, and understand the case fully. They are also muzzled.

Mowgli's owners were good people with good intent. They did no wrong. They were just very, very unlucky with the dog that they had chosen.

Sadly, Mowgli had had his last chance and I wrote a letter to his vet stating my views. The vet also agreed with our decision, having seen Mowgli's behaviour first hand in his surgery. So sadly, Mowgli was put to sleep a day later.

When I first 'got into' dogs, I used to think that when dogs went 'wrong' it was the fault of their owners. A long time ago in my naïvety I used to agree with the saying that 'there are no bad dogs, only bad owners'. But since then, so many years of experience have taught me that sadly, this is not always the case. I haven't seen many, but there have been a few that are simply unsuitable for living as a pet dog. Mowgli was one of them. Perhaps if Mowgli had been raised and worked as a livestock guarding breed, he might have been a good working dog, suited to life in the fields, protecting sheep from predators. He may have made a decent guard dog, or protection dog, or maybe something else. There may have been something in Mowgli's past that had made him how he was, but to me it looked like genetic behaviour in the wrong place: a domestic home.

★

I must commend Mowgli's owners for their enormous hearts and the kindness that they showed to him. They were very nice people and good, determined and committed owners, who wanted a happy life for their new canine friend. I do hope your hearts have healed.

I am sorry, Mowgli, that I could not help you. I hope that you are peaceful now. Run free.

Some days are just bad. That is how life is. For all of us. But there are other days with dogs that are, well, perfect!

Tomorrow could be a perfect day. I hoped so.

Cooper: A Perfect Day

It was the first day of my long-awaited holiday. Lace, Cloud, Connor and I were heading off to Wiltshire, to my spiritual home, to spend a whole week walking and relaxing. The first weekend there I had planned to meet a friend of many years. I'd not seen her for a long time and I was really looking forward to it. I arrived the day before we were due to meet, and having given the dogs a really good walk, settled down for a night in the caravan in beautiful ancient woodland that I have come to know over many years and which is one of my favourite places to be.

The following morning we got up early. Well, I did. I packed a rucksack, while the dogs helped by snoring in support. Then we set off for an early walk before my friend arrived.

It was a beautiful day, perfect for walking; sunny, warm but not too hot, and my spirits were soaring. We all seemed to be in high spirits as we walked through the enchanting ancient woodland with its twisted old trees and the sound of insects and birds. We watched squirrels flying from branch to branch, we heard birds calling, and overhead a buzzard circled and soared as it called out its wild cry. Everything seemed perfect.

Cloud, always up for an adventure, was up ahead of me and had been sniffing a bush. Then I saw her look up and back, behind me. She froze momentarily before relaxing somewhat and then sniffing the air. A moment behind her, the other two dogs having seen her behaviour change, also looked behind me and sniffed the air. They were fixated, so I looked to see what had got their attention.

Behind me, about seventy-five metres away, was a black-and-brown Collie-type dog. The dog had seen us all notice him. He paused, fixed still by our attention, and then he lowered his head and veered off to one side to sniff the ground. He knew that we had seen him but he did what he could to be polite by turning away and wandering off to one side. My dogs were interested in, but not concerned by, his presence. They knew that this dog presented no threat. I wondered momentarily where his owner was, but we all turned and wandered on again.

After a few paces I glanced over my shoulder and saw that he was trailing along behind us, following the same path that we were, but still no owner was in sight and nor could I hear anyone calling him. We continued our walk. But he had piqued my interest and in the apparent absence of an owner, also my concern.

Another fifty metres and I stopped again, and this time I turned around fully to see if he was still trailing us, or if I could see an owner. As I turned to observe him, he immediately stopped in his tracks, and ears and head raised, he stared straight at me momentarily before once again lowering his head and veering off to one side, and feigning disinterest by sniffing the ground. He looked a nice, polite, socially sophisticated dog. But surely he should be following his owner, not us!

Now I started to worry. It's not the first time that a dog has followed me and my dogs when out on a walk and I suspect it won't be the last. But we were miles from any inhabited place and I had the usual concerns about what is the best thing to do when being followed by someone else's dog.

I looked back again and he was closer still. Slowly, politely, it seemed he was intent on moving into our group and becoming part of our walk. I noticed at this point that he had no collar on.

After a few more metres, I stopped and turned to study him more clearly, and to think what to do. If he was lost, I didn't want to draw him from his owner, or his home. If he had no collar, then how could I return him to his owner? If he was microchipped then maybe I could, but not without taking him to a vet or rescue centre to have him checked for a chip. If he had no microchip then I suddenly had a dog I had no idea what to do with. Then what? The day had started to get more complicated.

Should I turn back and hope that we might find his owner? Should I get him to me and put a lead on him to keep him safe as we approached the part of the walk that ran near a road? Should I shoo him away and hope he might go home? Should I ring the police or find a dog warden? If I did, what would happen to him? A rescue centre? A new home? A needle? What to do, what to do… I decided to alter my course to avoid the busy road that might endanger him, and we continued.

I liked this dog. He was so polite in his attempt to join my little pack. He was a nice-looking animal with good manners and he seemed quite young. And what was more, my dogs seemed to accept his ever nearer attempts to join us. Why was that, I wondered? After following us for quite a few miles, he had somehow managed to become part of us.

A thought flashed into my mind. *Maybe I should take him and keep him?* I felt that I already liked him. He was following me, maybe it was meant to be?

It was a stupid idea. I simply could not take another dog into my life right now. With one really old dog and one really young one, *and* the almighty Cloud, I already had my hands more than full. I had no more spare time to train another dog. Or the money that his care might take. Or the energy to care for a fourth dog. And there was no more room in the car! *I could not take another dog into my life,* no matter what I felt for this dog. *No, Denise. No!* I told myself sternly.

Or could I?

For the next three hours the black-and-brown dog stuck with me and my dogs. And every moment he drew nearer. When we sat down to eat and I pulled my sandwiches from my rucksack, he too sat down a polite distance away.

He was now about three metres away and none of my dogs paid any attention whatsoever to his presence. As if they were totally accepting of him. He sat quietly, unassumingly. Waiting.

I had finished my sandwiches and there was some left over. I split the remainder into three, and then on reflection, four. Lace, Cloud, Connor, and yes, a little bit for the 'follower' too. I tossed him a bit of ham, which he approached with caution, but relished once he had checked that it was safe.

As I stood and put on my rucksack to continue the walk, all four dogs stood with me and all five of us walked on together. By now he was actually amongst my dogs and they seemed totally accepting of him, as if he belonged there. There was no sniffing or greeting, just quiet acceptance of his presence.

So he had joined our group. He copied the behaviour of the other dogs: when they strode forward, he went with them; when they slowed to sniff, he slowed too. He mimicked their every behaviour. He was seemingly desperate to fit in. And he did fit in.

For a short while he trotted ahead of me, with the other dogs, exploring the freshly laid scents of the woods that were all around us. As he was now plain in my sight, I observed his motion and became entranced by it. He sort of hovered over the ground, in his movement. A fluid, even motion that seemed without effort. He was a well-put-together animal and his gait was somehow soothing to me.

But where was his owner?

The walk continued without incident and the whole time my mind raced with thoughts about what to do with this dog with no collar. But my mind failed to conclude any answer. A few more miles and we were drawing near to the campsite. I called my dogs to me to have their leads on in accordance with the sensible campsite rules. I didn't have a spare lead for the black-and-brown dog, so I just hoped he would stay with me. He did, just following on with us, a few feet behind. He seemed to know that at this time, as my dogs were close to me, he should be close to me. I thought it was like he was just meant to be with us.

As I approached the site entrance, the two friendly campsite managers looked up and smiled at me. Ceasing the work they were doing, they turned to chat with me as they often did. Then the lady manager saw our new pack member trailing a few feet behind and her face looked sad for a moment, before she spoke.

"I see you've picked up the local stray. Poor thing, he is forever following people back here and we are forever calling his owner to retrieve him. One day he is going to get killed on that road." Her face fell into a frown and her arm waved toward the busy road at the end of the track, before she continued, "The man wants rid of him. I don't know why – he's a lovely dog. I'd like him, but my husband is allergic to dogs. Do you want him?"

A weird pang of sadness hit me as I realised two things. Firstly, the dog was unwanted by his owner even though he seemed a really lovely dog. And secondly, I had somehow come to think that there was some deeper meaning to him following me and my dogs. Living as I do in a head quite often full of unicorns and wishful thinking, I had come to believe that this dog and my dogs were somehow linked. I had come to think over the preceding hours that that was why he had followed us. I felt sad. He was not following *us,* he had just followed someone, anyone! It made me sad that such a well-mannered dog should feel the need to follow a stranger and her dogs. But mostly I just felt sad that he had an owner who apparently didn't care where his dog was.

"I will go get my phone and call his owner. Again." With a scowl on her face, the lady manager turned to walk away.

At that very moment, a car came up the track toward us. As it drew to a halt at the entrance barrier a few metres away, we all looked towards it. (That is what people who spend time on campsites do. They watch the incoming vehicles and their occupants. Each arrival is the beginning of a new story.) There, behind the steering wheel was my friend, Jenny. She was beaming and waving at me frantically. Over her shoulder I could see the black-and-white face of her own Collie, Cameron, swaying from side to side with what must have been a wagging tail in response to seeing me and my dogs. The car halted abruptly, she jumped out and arms wide, face still beaming, she ran the few paces toward me. I smiled inside and out to see her – it had been too long!

She hugged me hard as I hugged her and then, having seen him over my shoulder, she stepped back, pushed me away a little and turned her attention instead to the seemingly more interesting black-and-brown dog who was hovering a few metres away. Sounding delighted she said, "Dee, oh Dee, you have a new dog! Why didn't you tell me? What a surprise! He's lovely!"

The dog regarded her from the short distance, without undue concern. We all stood and watched in silence as Jenny took centre stage. She leant forward slightly, turned her body to one side somewhat, patted her thigh, and in so doing, invited the dog into her space. The young dog responded to her invite.

"What's his name?" she enquired as she leant down to touch the dog who drew slowly and politely toward her. I looked at the campsite manager for an answer. Did she know his name? Her face was blank.

I began to explain to my friend. "He isn't mine, Jenny. He just decided to follow us home when I was out walking this morning. He followed us for miles, all the way here. Apparently, his owner doesn't care for him much and wants rid of him."

Jenny's voice was fever pitch with excitement: "I'll have him!"

All heads turned to Jenny. "You will?" I said, surprised but yet suddenly elated.

"Yes, he is lovely and I've been looking for a new dog for a few weeks now. Can I have him? He looks perfect. Do you think he will make a good agility dog, Dee?"

I looked at the campsite manager to see a broad smile spread across her face. I looked at the dog I'd known just a few hours and considered his good posture and his straight, forward-pointing legs. I remembered the way he had seemingly floated above the ground once in motion, and I figured that yes, he might well make a good agility dog.

Jenny I knew to be an excellent dog owner. Fond of long-distance walks and a keen agility competitor, and I had seen Jenny thoroughly love and care for several dogs in her lifetime, mostly Collies. I knew also that even if he didn't become a keen agility dog, he would still have a life of love and care with this experienced owner. She would find something that he would love to do and make sure he had chances to do it.

"Well, I will ring his owner and find out!" said the campsite manager, beaming, and went off to get her phone. Returning a few moments later, smiling broadly, she said the owner was on his way now, with the dog's bowl and lead. Jenny smiled ecstatically and went off to her car for a moment, and the dog started to follow her. She returned with a slip lead. Leaning forward again, she called to the dog to come to her. "Come on, little fella." The dog's tail flipped a few wags as he approached and as he arrived in front of her, he raised his muzzle slowly toward her, then he turned and sat on her foot, leaning against her leg, desperate for her touch. Gently she slipped the leash over his head, stroked his neck with affection and the deal was done. Jenny had the new dog she had been looking for and the unwanted dog was suddenly a wanted dog, set for a very happy and well-cared-for life.

The dog's old owner arrived twenty minutes later and as the car drew up the track toward us, the dog with no name recognised it and he leaned into his new lead, *trying to pull away* from the car and from his old owner. My heart raged with anger at this man that I didn't know, whose dog apparently did not want to go home with him. I didn't want to think about why that was. But the anger was overridden by the joy I now knew that this dog was about to feel in his new home – a loving, experienced home.

The man passed a water bowl and a lead with a collar attached to Jenny. Both lead and collar looked as if they had never been used. He said simply, "His name is Cooper." Without even glancing at the dog he had just given away, he turned and walked away from us, got into his car, and drove off. I was so happy. His old owner had gone and a new life awaited this lovely dog.

For the rest of his life, Cooper was loved. He was well cared-for and walked twice daily. He swam often and he went on to be an enthusiastic agility dog. I revelled in seeing photos of him on Facebook and we met and walked together as often as we could. Jenny's other dog loved him too, as did mine, and I have rarely seen a happier, more contented dog anywhere.

It was a day that started perfectly and ended even more perfectly, for Cooper.

Some days are just utterly brilliant!

Gladys

Now and again a dog or owner comes along who changes your view about many things and teaches you something you never even knew you didn't know. A dog like Gladys, and her owner, Sarah.

It was week one of another puppy course. As the owners began to arrive with their new puppies, it was evident that there was the usual mix of pride and fear amongst the owners and excitement and nerves amongst puppies. There were common breeds, a variety of Border Collies, German Shepherds, Spaniels, the odd 'continental breed', an Akita, and then there was Gladys, an English Bull Terrier.

English Bull Terriers with their strange, curious Roman noses are one of those breeds that just didn't usually appeal to me. But this little pup was such a character that she made me smile and gasp in admiration. She was all play bows and wagging tails as she watched all the pups come in and she was just as waggy and pleased to see all the people too. Quite unusual for the breed.

As she approached the registration desk she looked happy and relaxed and her owner was smiling and gushing with pride. "I've always wanted an English Bull Terrier and Gladys is just such fun. I love her so much!" she told me whilst I chatted to her as she checked in. I light up inside when I can see an owner who just adores their dog and a dog who adores its owner in equal measure. I was looking forward to working with this combination from the moment I saw them together.

Gladys sure was a character, and over the next few months I grew to love her and her owner too. Sarah was one of those owners who goes home with her homework, practises like mad, and comes back the next week much further advanced than all the other puppies and owners. She was a smiling, upbeat, positive, laughing lady who found happiness in nearly every event and she always had a humorous quip and slant on everything, making her a joy to work with. Gladys seemed to have become infected with her owner's positivity and was confident for her breed. She shone, seemingly with the sheer enjoyment of life.

And then, when Gladys was nine months, *it* happened.

Sarah rang to say that Gladys had come into season and asked if she needed to stay away from the group until the season had passed. I advised her that we usually asked them to stay away for three full weeks of classes. We chatted about her progress and soon the phone call ended. I knew that I would miss them in class, but looked forward to seeing them again soon.

When she returned, the class started as normal with me asking everyone if they had any questions or had had any problems that we needed to talk about before we started training. I also asked if they had learnt anything new that they wanted to show off. Gladys's owner, looking a little concerned, said that she had a video that she wished to show me later, after class. She went on to show us her new tricks and as we watched Gladys go through the repertoire that she had learnt in her longer than usual absence, everyone was smiling in admiration of her.

But as I watched I couldn't help but feel that something wasn't quite right with Gladys; I wondered what the video her owner had taken might show me. I couldn't quite put my finger on what was different, just that she *was* different somehow. Maybe a little more aloof, a little less attentive to Sarah? Maybe the season had matured her, as seasons usually do, out of some of her puppyness?

Class came and went and as people filed out of the door, I went over to Gladys's owner to watch the video and learn more.

Sarah tapped her phone as she began to explain. "About two weeks into her season, she started to chase her tail like this, and she has done it more and more often and it's really hard to stop her," she told me. Dark mood and concern were evident on her face as she relived a memory. I'd never seen her frown before: she was such a positive, upbeat lady.

Chasing tails is a common enough thing. Sometimes caused by boredom, sometimes attention seeking, sometimes it has been inadvertently rewarded or sometimes it can be a sign of anal gland problems, skin irritations or various other issues. I doubted in Gladys's case if it was boredom or attention seeking, so I thought maybe anal gland problems? Usually easy enough to resolve. I wasn't too worried by what she had told me.

She held out her phone for me to watch and as I did, my heart sank to the bottom of my boots. I simply couldn't understand what I was seeing. The dog on the screen in front of me looked nothing like the Gladys I knew! She didn't actually appear to be chasing her tail as such. Instead she seemed to be just spinning round and round, in a frantic, obsessive, high speed whirl of activity. As I watched I grew increasingly uncomfortable in my stomach. Then a few minutes in I realised that as she span, she was also drifting across the room.

In her fixated frenzy, she was heading for some large wooden furniture. The sound was playing on the phone and I heard Sarah's sister, who was off screen, frantically calling to Gladys, trying desperately to distract her and get her away from the furniture as she span, whilst her owner continued to film the impending impact to show to me.

BANG! Her head slammed into the solid frame of the dresser, she staggered for a second, but then the spinning recommenced, as if the impact had not occurred. Even for the Bull Terrier breed that must have really hurt – she could have broken her neck – but she just kept on spinning. Round and round and round she went, as if her life depended on it.

The video went on and on with Gladys's spinning showing no signs of abatement. Several more minutes into the video, I asked how long this went on for. I was advised that it had been over an hour on that occasion and that this was not the worst incident. Last night she had spun for several hours until eventually, with raw and bleeding paws, she had collapsed, exhausted.

I looked down at Gladys's feet: they were all red.

I didn't know what to say. The fact that she had banged head-first into the cupboard door, a solid object, but that it had not deterred her in any way and the spinning had continued concerned me greatly. I'd never seen a dog so committed to an activity that a hard bang to its head had passed unnoticed.

I switched the video back on and watched some more. As I watched I could see that she held something in her mouth and that her jaw seemed locked tight around it. The speed of the spin prevented me from seeing the object clearly so I paused it and watched in slow motion. As I did, I grew even more uneasy. The whites of her eyes were showing, her pupils dilated – they looked like black holes – windows into a demented soul. She looked demonic, absent, frightening in her intensity.

It looked like a small feather that she held in her mouth. I wondered briefly if the feather had some kind of toxin on it that had infected her. But it wasn't always a feather that caused the spinning, I was told, so I ruled that one out.

We stood and chatted for well over an hour as I established the facts. Her owner's face had changed from the smiley laughing face I had come to know. Darkness now clouded her eyes as she recounted her experience.

Sarah said that when they had once tried to intervene physically to stop Gladys spinning it had resulted in a bite to her sister and that they dare not risk it again. I was stunned. Gladys? Biting a human? Really? She was just not that sort of dog!

It seems that Gladys only started spinning when she had something in her mouth. So over the next few weeks, we spoke on the phone many times and I came up with as many ideas as I could to stop her getting things in her mouth, or prevent or interrupt the spinning.

We tried muzzling her when she was not on-lead or she was left unattended, so she couldn't pick up anything in her mouth. But she soon learnt to push her nose to the ground so that she could grasp the basket muzzle with her front teeth and start to spin. The muzzling failed. So we tried caging her in a small covered cage, too small to spin in, whilst I spent time ringing training friends and researching what I could about the condition. The vet tried anti-convulsant drugs and sedatives, which made her sleep more, but once awake, she started to spin. I suggested giving her a large cow's femur bone so she could gnaw for hours, hoping the love of bones might keep her from spinning. After stripping the meat off it, she picked up the huge bone and began to spin with it. She smashed into things in the garden with the giant bone and broke one of her own teeth. After speaking with a canine nutrition expert we changed her diet; the behaviour didn't change. We tried interrupting it with a loud noise, but she seemed not to hear it. Then we tried increasing her exercise by taking her on bike rides, but they didn't get far before she grasped her muzzle and began to spin. We increased her training, but there is only so much time you can spend training each day.

Throughout this time I went in search of information and help. And what I discovered worried me. Spinning was, I soon learnt, a common and recognised behaviour problem in the breed. Though I had never encountered it before, it often began as many behaviour problems do at adolescence. Though many dogs of this breed were 'spinners', for most the behaviour was considered harmless, but for others, like Gladys, it had become more serious and had been accompanied with other behaviour changes, like the biting.

Learned behaviours can be unlearned; genetic behaviours are much harder to deal with.

There was a research programme in the US and I wrote to them explaining the case and asking for help. I didn't receive a reply and later realised that the programme had closed a few years earlier. The more I looked, the more I realised that this was probably going to be beyond me to resolve. I just didn't have relevant experience or know what to do. Furthermore, I didn't know anyone who could help. Despite many phone calls and emails over several weeks, none of my experienced dog-training friends could offer anything beyond what we had already tried. My heart began to feel very low indeed.

A few weeks later Gladys was back in class and she seemed distant, aloof and like a shadow of her former self. She seemed content to work in class though, so her owner was keen to keep bringing her, as it was the only time she didn't seem to want to spin. Her paws looked so sore I wondered if she should be even taking part in class, but I knew if I sent her home, she was probably destined for more spinning. At the end of class, we stood and chatted. Gladys stood calmly beside her owner.

I heard my phone ring from the desk a few metres behind me. One of my friends kindly answered it for me and called my name to get my attention to the phone call waiting, "Denise!" and I turned towards them. As I turned my back on her, Gladys leapt up very high and grabbed my shoulder in her teeth. The bite came from nowhere. Neither of us saw it coming. I looked at my shoulder: it would be bruised and there were teeth marks, but the skin wasn't broken. Gladys had dropped to the floor and stood looking at me. I couldn't read her expression but for the first time, I felt scared of her. Sarah began to cry. I wanted to cry too as I realised that Gladys was now too unpredictable and too dangerous for me to have her continue in classes. My heart sank as I realised that I couldn't help her anymore. I just didn't know what to do next.

Out of sheer desperation, I suggested that she contact the dog's breeder to see if there was anything they could suggest and find out if other related animals had the same problem. It would buy me more time, though what I would do with that time I had no idea. I had come to the end of the road. None of my training or behaviour friends, or my vets, could suggest anything we had not already tried. Sarah's face brightened and she smiled briefly. "What a good idea!"

She rang me later in better spirits to say that the breeder had been pretty relaxed about it and had said, "Oh, it's not a problem. Her mother does it too. Several of our dogs do it. I can see her mother spinning in the kennel right now as we speak. Just bring her back to us and we will sort her out."

"*Oh, it's not a problem.*" The words haunted me. The breeder of this dog thought that this dangerous and frightening behaviour was not a problem. Alarms bells began to ring in my mind. But what else could we do? Sarah sounded relieved that she had found someone who thought that the issue was not serious. She admitted to needing a break from Gladys whilst she gathered her own peace back up. Her life had been controlled completely by Gladys's recent behaviour problems and Sarah was exhausted from the worry and lack of sleep. She felt guilty, but relieved, that she was to have a few days' rest whilst the breeder 'sorted out' Gladys.

She took Gladys back to the breeder on the agreement that they would have her for a week. They met at the same halfway point that she had picked Gladys up from as a tiny puppy. A motorway service station. The breeder lived hundreds of miles away.

★

Two days later, Sarah rang me again. I recognised the number on the phone and I had mixed emotions as I answered. I really liked Sarah and Gladys too, they were both great, but I still felt anxiety at the thought of what was about to come. I hit the answer button. "Hi Sarah. How are things?"

She was sobbing. Eventually she started to form words and speak slowly. "It's… Gladys." More sobs. "You have to look at the website." Between sobs and sniffles, she read out a website address and I wrote it down.

She gasped for breath, tried to steady her voice, before continuing, "I can't talk about it. Sorry." And then she hung up.

I stared at the phone. I wondered if I could bear whatever I might see on the website.

I fired up my computer and keyed in the address. There, at the top of the page, was a picture of Gladys, the dog I knew so well, standing with her tail held out by a hand in a show stance. She looked a fine animal, but her feet still looked very sore.

Over the picture were four words I could hardly comprehend, in bold: **"GORGEOUS PUPPY FOR SALE."**

The words below read:

SADIE. Pure bred pedigree English Bull Terrier puppy from top show line stock, sadly up for re-homing. Only six months old and coming into top condition, this poor dog has been badly let down by her former owner, who had no time for her, so she needs a new home. Very friendly, she is great with children and other dogs and will make a fine family pet, house dog, or a show dog. Will you give this poor dog a home?

Price: £800

Safe with children? Only six months old? A fine family pet? After the bite she had delivered to me I didn't consider her safe with anyone, let alone children. Her spinning was dangerous, not to mention the even more worrying unprovoked and sudden attack on me and the bite to Sarah's sister! I had an image in my mind of Gladys spinning and knocking over a small child and the child screaming in fear and in pain. I saw blood spurt from the imaginary child's head as she hit the wall, hard. She wasn't safe with even me; no way was she a family pet prospect, not until the problem was resolved.

I just stared at the screen. I couldn't believe it.

And then from deep inside, grew an uncontrollable rage. I was fuming at their use of the words 'badly let down by her former owner'. Sarah had been a brilliant, committed owner. I was horrified at the prospect of this dog being put in any unsuspecting home, let alone one with children in it. I had to take action.

I scrolled down, found the phone number and punched it into my phone.

It rang, and a woman answered.

"Hello," I said as calmly as I could, "I am ringing about the dog you have advertised on your website."

"Oh, poor Sadie. Yes, she is still for sale." I could read no emotion at all in the voice. Surely she must feel guilty?

I delved to find out more. "Can you tell me a bit more about her, please?"

"Her first owner didn't treat her very well, poor thing. Just left her shut away in a room all the time."

The anger started to consume me.

"She is good with dogs and friendly with children too. I can send more photos. Where do you live? We can deliver her for you. Do you want her?"

Do I want her? She didn't even know anything about me, yet she was willing to deliver her, no questions asked. I guess that is what I should have expected after the lies I'd read in the advert.

Rage coursed through me and for one of only a few times in my professional career, I completely lost it. The emotion rushed out of me as accompaniment to the words. Fury paved each sentence. "How could you say these things? I am the dog's trainer; I've known her from a puppy. Her name is Gladys, not Sadie. Her owner was brilliant, the dog has serious problems. She isn't safe. How could you re-home her? I am horrified at what you're doing. The owner has not signed her over to you – she isn't even yours to sell! I am going to complain to the highest levels. I will contact the Kennel Club, ring the police, I am going to spread your name all over the internet, I am going to—"

She hung up.

I rang back several times but the phone said, "Sorry this number is not available, please try later." In my rage I fired off an email, threatening all sorts of things. I had to make them stop. Gladys could not be re-homed with children. She wasn't even theirs to sell: Sarah had not signed her over, she was simply hoping they would help her. She had never known where they lived and she had been too upset, after she saw the advert, to ring them. She had left it to me.

So I decided to take further action. I went back to look for the address of the breeder and I intended to go round there and get the dog back, even if I had to steal her.

I keyed in the web address once more, intent on visiting the breeder the next day as a fake buyer.

"URL not found." The website had gone.

The phone number was unobtainable, the website gone. I had nowhere left to go.

I did contact the Kennel Club, but what could they do? There was seemingly nothing that anyone could do.

★

Over the next few days, Sarah and I spoke several more times, when she had calmed down enough to stop sobbing. I felt so much guilt that it was me who had suggested she contact the breeder. I felt I had consigned Gladys to... well, to goodness only knows what. I could not imagine any good outcomes for poor Gladys let alone any unsuspecting family who may have bought her. Sarah and I were both reeling from the shock and at a loss as to what to do, but at least it seemed that she didn't blame me. We just didn't know what to do next.

Tragically, neither Sarah nor I ever found out what happened to Gladys and a little bit of my heart, and hers, was consigned to darkness, forever.

It was a case that nearly finished my dog career. The straw that very nearly broke my dog-training back. Yes I had helped many thousands of dogs for sure, but now and again, a single case came along that made me want to just walk away from it all. To leave someone else to help the dogs and owners that

I no longer felt strong enough, or able enough, to help. On a whim, I applied for a job as a van delivery driver. I didn't get the job. Partially disheartened, and partially relieved, I remained in dog training.

★

But happily, Sarah's story didn't end there. Some months later Sarah called me again. "Hi Denise, it's Sarah, with…" Her voice trailed off for a moment. She had always introduced herself as "Sarah, with Gladys." I heard her take a sharp intake of breath as she composed herself at the memory, before continuing, "It's Sarah, from Lincoln." *No longer Gladys's owner.*

"I found a little dog locked in a wooden box, in a ditch down the lane where I live. She's a little scrap of a thing, was riddled with worms and fleas, very underweight and fearful. Looks like a young German Shepherd cross, I think. She is lovely and so sweet. No one knows who she is so I am keeping her. Can I come back to classes please? I've named her Hope."

I was delighted to welcome Sarah and Hope to classes. Once more this lively, committed, talented owner had a dog to love and to train, and over the coming months we worked to turn Hope around. Within a few weeks her fear had mostly gone, she gained weight, her coat began to shine, good health was restored by good food, care and exercise, and very soon, once again, Sarah was demoing tricks and obedience skills to us all and was leading the class to new levels with her enthusiasm and dedication. They were a delight to be with and little Hope was one of those dogs that just fills you with smiles. The love between them shone and it was a total joy to see the transformation that unravelled in front of us each week.

For Sarah and Hope, at least there was a happy ending.

★

To anyone thinking of buying any breed, I strongly urge you to look into any genetically based behaviour problems that might be prevalent in your breed of choice before buying a puppy. If any breeder offers to 'deliver' a puppy to you, knowing nothing about you, having asked you no questions, then this is not a caring breeder. If they care not where their puppies go and deliver a pup to you, effectively preventing you from seeing the dog's parents in their homes, then they probably care not what problems the puppy might have.

Stay away from such breeders, and in so doing, you will dry up their income and you can instead support good breeders, of which there are many, who quiz their potential puppy buyers, who have taken care to avoid genetic faults, who actually care about the animals they are producing and the lives that those animals are to lead.

Good breeders *are* out there: I hope that you find one of them.

★

So much time has passed that whatever happened to Gladys at the breeder's, she must now be over the rainbow bridge.

To Gladys, wherever you are. I am so sorry that I could not help you and that I let you down. I hope that you are happy and well now, and that one day, I will see you again. Please know that you were much loved, if not fully understood. We miss you.

I'm sorry. Run free.

Tiny Tink

When I first met Tink he was just twelve weeks old and had come to join my puppy classes. He was the smallest twelve-week-old puppy I had ever seen, by quite some way.

On his registration form his breed was stated as Teacup Chihuahua. I had heard of the 'teacup' trend but at that time had yet to encounter it first hand. I just couldn't get over how tiny and dainty he was, as if with one breath of wind and he might just fly off, like a plastic bag caught in an updraft. I noted that his teeny amber-coloured paws were smaller than my little fingernail. As he trotted on the floor in dog class he made a delicate tip-tapping sound, like a small bird makes on a table top when it's picking up crumbs.

I was weirdly entranced by this palm-sized dog-shaped bundle of fun and energy. No matter how much I looked at him, I couldn't get how such a small thing could actually be a fully functioning dog. Yet in many ways he was just like any other dog.

Tink's owners were first-time dog owners and had come to classes to "learn all we can about dogs and to have Tink as well trained and behaved as we can, so we can take him everywhere with us," as they had told me. A pleasant, often smiling and laughing young couple, what they lacked in experience they more than made up for in both enthusiasm and commitment. Throughout the two courses they spent with us (twelve weeks), they listened attentively, worked hard on the exercises, were happy and fun to be with in class, and clearly loved Tink to bits.

Tink was somewhat aloof with the bigger dogs and tried hard to keep out of their way. But all the dogs at class had known Tink since they were small puppies, so even as they grew much bigger, they understood that Tink was not overly playful and they left him be. Whilst he continued to avoid big dogs, he did make a couple of friends with two other small, gentle puppies. And to all intents and purposes, all was going well.

Tink's owners told me that they would be leaving at the end of the course as they were moving over 300 miles away, down to the seaside to work and to live. The seaside! You lucky, lucky people! I wanted to be moving to the seaside with them! So I wished them well.

I was definitely very sad to see Tink and his owners go. They were lovely people and I had this weird obsession with studying Tink. I wondered what might happen after he left. I wondered if I might be compelled to go and buy one of these tiny dogs, to continue my obsession. Stranger things have happened in my life, that's for sure!

He had done well enough in class and had dedicated owners, and was of such a nature and character that I foresaw no behaviour problems in the making with Tink, so I didn't ever expect to see him again.

Feeling disappointed inside I bade farewell to tiny Tink. "Bye Tink," I waved to him sadly as he left the room for the last time. Trotting out the door toward his new life, by the sea, head held high, attentive and bright as he always was, as he left my life.

★

But just two months later, he was back. His owners were on the phone to me. "Denise, Jenny and James here with Tink. Do you remember us?" She sounded worried.

How could I forget? My heart warmed to hear her voice and Tink's name and then it clouded over when I began to wonder what was wrong with Tink and why they had rung me. I greeted her and told her that yes, I most definitely remembered them. She told me that they had a problem with Tink that meant it was too scary to take him out. "We've been all over the place trying to get help with it down here, but no one can explain it or seems to know what to do, so we thought we had better talk to you." For a few seconds, my mind went wild trying to guess what was going to be the problem with Tink. I had no idea. She continued in a breathless rush.

"Dogs keep picking up Tink and running off with him. It's happened twice in the last week or so. In the local park a dog just ran up to him, picked him up and carried him off. James and me and the dog's owner ran after him, the dog that stole Tink, but the dog wouldn't drop him and he just kept running and he was avoiding us and the whole time Tink was in his mouth and, and…" her voice was getting higher as she relived the panic-struck moments in her mind, but still she didn't pause for a breath, "… we didn't even know if Tink was still alive in his mouth, and the dog went right off across the park with us running behind and it was terrifying and horrifying and we thought he was going to be dead…"

She paused to take a breath at last; she heaved as she filled her lungs and as she tried to calm the emotions that ran through her as she relived the horrible experience she had had. That of Tink being taken away by what turned out to be a much larger mastiff dog. I cringed too at the image in my own mind.

I asked her a few questions about what had happened, immediately before and after the incident, and how they had got Tink out of the big dog's mouth in the end. Tink had been running towards her in the park, she told me. The mastiff-type dog had just run in from the side, picked Tink up whilst he was mid-run and ran off with him in his mouth. At first Tink had squealed, but then his squealing had stopped after a few hundred metres and for a while, the owners had thought that he must surely be dead. But they still chased the big dog in the hope of at least retrieving Tink's body.

My gut clenched with sympathy – what a horrid thing for them to have lived through. All of them, the mastiff's owners too, must have been horrified.

Eventually the four people had managed to corner the mastiff between a wall and a fence and then the dog's owners had persuaded him to let go of Tink in exchange for some sausage they had in their pocket. Amazingly, Tink had been totally uninjured.

The larger dog's owners had been extremely upset, said their dog had done nothing like this before and having apologised profusely, offered to pay for vet bills. The vet later concluded that there was no damage whatsoever to Tink, and Tink himself had seemed unfazed by the whole thing. He had shown no signs of fear when he next met a big dog; just his usual polite avoidance.

They chalked it up to bad luck, decided to keep a lookout for the mastiff in future and had committed to keeping a watchful eye over any dog in the park that might be a risk to Tink. The mastiff's owners, also shocked, had decided they needed to get some help for their dog too.

But then a week later, it had happened again. Tink had been running loose in the park, and then just like before a dog had come running after him, picked him up in its mouth and started to run off across the field, away from its owner's recalls. Once more they found themselves in hot pursuit of the little dog they loved who was inside the mouth of a dog they didn't know – this time a Labrador.

The Labrador eventually came to a halt after much shouting from her owner and looking submissive and coy, she said, the dog had conceded to drop Tink, unharmed, on the floor. She thought the Labrador looked as if she knew she had done wrong.

As she continued, I became more bemused. "Funny thing was, as soon as the dog had dropped Tink, it showed no interest in him again. Just like the other dog. It was like they didn't want to pick him up again, they just lost interest. Why would they do that?"

That question set my mind a-buzzing. *Yes, why would they do that?*

In all my years, I had never had anyone ring me and tell me of such an incident. A hundred thoughts ran though my mind. Had they seen Tink as a toy? Had they been incited to chase because he was small and running? Did they see him as prey because of his size? Why hadn't they hurt him? Why was he not bothered by either incident that had traumatised his owners so? Why had the other dogs involved run away from their owners, not toward them? Had that been a deliberate act? If so, did that mean that they didn't see him as a toy but as prey? Or did it mean they were just not retrieve or recall trained? Why did they lose interest in him? Was it something to do with chase sequence?

In the end, I concluded that I just didn't know.

"The thing is," she said, "we want Tink to be a normal dog, and do normal dog things, despite his small size. He has made friends with some dogs in the park and likes to play, and he never gets angry with other dogs, unless they tread on him. If he doesn't know them he just avoids them. But we can't bear to see this happen again. Do you think it was just bad luck?"

She and I were both silent for a minute and then she asked the 'impossible to answer for sure' question: "Do you think it will happen again?" And another impossible, even harder to answer question: "Can you make it stop?"

I just didn't know.

★

When I listen to a person tell me the history of their dog, and I consider the facts as we know them, sometimes things are just obvious. Some problems you see over and over again. 'Jumping up people' is a good example. Nearly always caused by the same thing, nearly always solved in one of a few ways, and very easily preventable if you start when the dog is still a puppy. Some dog behaviour is so obvious in its pattern that it is easy to see how it came to develop and how to solve it, or prevent it.

But some behaviour is not that simple.

In my experience, a single bad event can sometimes be just a single bad event. It can be just bad luck, or due to an unfortunate set of circumstances. One-offs do occur. But when the exact same thing happens more than once, especially if the two events are close in time, then that is not bad luck, that is the start of a pattern. A pattern of behaviour tells me a lot more than one-off circumstances. It tells me that unless something changes, then it is likely to happen again. "If nothing changes, nothing changes" (original author thought to be Shawn Anderson – thank you).

But on this occasion I had never even seen this problem before, let alone begun to understand the driver behind the seeming pattern of behaviour that was developing. So I had no idea at all what to do about it. Or whether I could do anything about it.

Sometimes you just can't go on the facts of the case; *sometimes you can go only on what you can see for yourself or what you feel.* I needed to see Tink. To watch him and to see what I noticed and be there, to see if anything came to me. And what's more, on this occasion I was going to really need some help to understand this case, from someone who knew much more about dogs than I did. Only a dog can tell us how a dog views another dog. So that somebody had to be canine.

I arranged for Tink and his owners to come to meet with me and all three of my dogs.

I was both excited and troubled the day that Tink came. I'd had sleepless nights trying to think, and think again. But nothing had come to me other than the random thoughts that I'd already had.

We all met up outside the training centre with all four dogs. I had my three dogs at my side, on their leads. They had Tink on his lead.

Cloud was the dog that I was really focused on; she was the wise one and the one I felt confident would help me. Connor was my more gentle and very handsome back-up plan, and Mirk was just there because he was so damn lovely to be around and he didn't like being left out. Plus he would be very helpful if we needed a dog to make friends with Tink for any reason. Mirk was gentler than a lamb.

My dogs showed enough interest to sniff the air and assess Tink, but then lost interest and looked at me to see what we were going to do. We walked together up the field, and my dogs took no notice of Tink. We went faster, trotting along side by side, and still no reaction from my dogs. They had accepted him into our group and soon were totally relaxed with him. Their reactions had told me nothing and I was still baffled.

In both cases Tink had been running when the incidents occurred, so I set up a recall. With my dogs on-lead and in full sight of the recall test, I asked Tink's owners to recall him. Tink responded well and trotted back to his calling owner. There was no response from my dogs other than passing interest.

Hmmmmm. Had they really driven all this way for me to come up with no explanation and to offer no solution?

We repeated it. Another recall, this time toward the other owner. Again Tink trotted off happily and my dogs watched him go, then looked back at me.

What are we doing here? they seemed to ask.

I enquired some more about the circumstances at the time of the attack, clutching at the hope that I had missed something that might help. I discovered that they had been calling Tink from a very long way away.

Maybe that was it? Maybe Tink was so far away from his owners at the time that the other dog had felt he might be a toy with no owner, or a lone prey animal, or… well, something else. What was I missing? What were my dogs missing? Had it really been two one-offs?

So while Tink's 'dad' (James) held his lead, I sent Jenny to the very far side of the field and asked her to do a long recall. With my dogs still on leads, we stood and watched. Tink watched Jenny head off across the field and he grew frustrated and began to pull on his lead. At a distance of about 150 yards, she called him and James released him.

This time, due to the distance his owner had gone and the subsequent frustration that had been created in Tink, once he was released he leapt forward at top speed, straight into a canter rather than the trot he had done previously.

The moment he did, Cloud and Connor lunged forward on their leads, without barking, and had they been free I am quite sure they would have pursued him. They looked predatory, heads lower than usual, and they were full of intent. I had never seen either dog behave this way toward another dog before and I watched in amazement.

Stranger than that, though, was what happened inside my own mind. At the exact same moment they lunged, my own brain presented me with an image of the running Tink as a rabbit, not a dog. I *saw* a rabbit in my mind.

The way a human 'sees' is a fascinating thing in itself. What we see in our head is actually our own brain's interpretation of what our eyes have seen. My brain thought that because this small animal was moving like a rabbit, it was a rabbit, and that is what I 'saw'. Presumably that is what happened to my dogs too. It was one of the most bizarre visual trick experiences I have ever had.

Curiously, the moment Cloud and Connor had lunged forward on their leads, old Mirk on the other hand had not. Was his eyesight so poor that he couldn't see well enough? Was his brain working off smell and not vision? 'Rabbit? What rabbit?' Bless him. Or was it that Mirk was just a less predatory animal then my other two? Or maybe Mirk (who I had only owned since he was eleven years old) had never seen a rabbit in motion, so his brain couldn't match the image with that of a rabbit? Certainly in the years I had known him, I had never seen him attempt to chase a rabbit or a squirrel or any other 'prey'. In fact, though he had been a top-class sheepdog for many years, I had observed that he wasn't really that bothered about working sheep either. He did what he was told to do, but if he was loose in a field full of sheep, he would show no interest in them at all unless he was told to. He was compliant and had herding instincts, but he would sooner just have a sleep than work sheep. Or was it that he had just been looking the wrong way when Tink had set off? I didn't know.

As I continued to observe Tink as he ran toward his owner, my brain began to make more sense of the image and the vision of a rabbit started to transform back into that of a dog. It was a very strange experience. As I continued to watch I observed that Tink's motion pattern at canter was almost identical to that of a rabbit. His front feet hit the ground one after the other, as all normal dogs do, but then his back legs had sort of 'hopped' together, like a rabbit does. Add this pattern of motion to the fact that he had large sticky-up ears and I could completely see he how he had been mistaken for a rabbit by the dogs that had previously picked him up.

This would also explain why the dogs who had lifted Tink up had lost interest in him when they had been made to drop him – because Tink had not been running anymore, they didn't think he was a rabbit.

Did it also explain why they had not hurt Tink? Perhaps when they saw him run they were incited to chase the 'rabbit', but once he was in their mouth, he smelt and presumably tasted like a dog? Both sets of owners had reported that their dogs had never picked up any other dog, or been aggressive or predatory toward any other dog.

My dogs lost interest in Tink as soon as he reached Jenny and ceased running. Then they looked back at me, wondering what we were doing next. Meanwhile old Mirk, who had lain down a few moments earlier, began snoring loudly. As Jenny walked back toward us with Tink trotting at her side, neither dog took any notice.

I had never encountered anything like this before and I could not be 100 per cent certain that I was right in my thinking. I am still not 100 per cent sure, but I did think that given the response of my dogs and the weird image I had 'seen' of a rabbit that it was not safe for Tink to be allowed to run fast in the presence of dogs that didn't know him. Perhaps his dog friends knew him well enough to know he was a dog even when he ran like a rabbit, but sadly, I felt in my heart, it was very likely that Tink would be picked up by another dog again if he were allowed to run free with dogs he didn't know.

I began to relay my thoughts to Tink's owners, telling them what I had 'seen' in my own mind, and I explained about the motor patterns of different types of animals and that my dogs had never lunged at a dog in the way they just had done to Tink – I believed they too had 'seen' a rabbit.

Although his owners were disappointed with my conclusion, they understood what I had said and had even, I later discovered, had the same thoughts on a previous occasion: they had commented to each other that from a distance, Tink looked like a rabbit to them too.

It was decided that for his own safety Tink be withdrawn from off-leash running in public places where there might be other dogs who didn't know him. They had joined a training class in their new town and had a big garden that Tink could run and play ball in, so Tink's life was still one of fulfilment, and we all considered that he was safe to be walked in public on-lead, as long as he didn't run.

★

And so it was that once again, Tink left my life. Again I waved sadly as he walked off back to his new life. And I went on with dog training, equipped with new knowledge about how dogs see dogs and how dogs see prey animals.

It wasn't a totally satisfactory outcome for Tink's owners or for me, but it was one that I felt had the best chance of keeping Tink safe.

Have fun Tink, and stay safe, little fella.

Cloud: Be Careful What You Wish For

In 2003, I decided to get my first puppy. I had already been teaching puppy owners for several years in classes and although I'd lived with a boyfriend's puppy and had close experience of many friends having puppies, some of whom had boarded temporarily with me, I'd never actually owned a puppy and watched it grow as my own. I'd never experienced the ongoing daily challenges that my customers experienced. So I felt I owed it to them to learn more about puppy ownership.

Having always had older, ex-shelter dogs, this was a new and exciting time for me. I had thought long and hard what I wanted a new dog for, what I wanted to do with it and what sort of dog I would prefer.

Once I had established those facts in my mind I said them out loud to my then boyfriend: "I've decided I want a puppy this time. It needs to be a Border Collie as I'd love to train another sheepdog. But the most important thing is that it is bold, confident and tenacious enough to be capable of doing either/and agility, obedience, heelwork to music, working trials or sheep work. I need a dog who can cope with whatever I throw at her in terms of training. I also really want, though this is least important, a dog that is striking to look at. It must be a bitch and one who will challenge me and teach me things

169

that no other dog has taught me. I want to learn more, and all I can, about dogs!"

I've always believed that knowing what you really want is the hard part, but once you say it out loud, the universe has a funny way of providing it. My boyfriend agreed I needed a strong, flexible dog and we both smiled at the thought of a cute, fluffy little puppy coming into our lives. A puppy! How exciting. And so the search for a puppy began.

Five days later I had a phone call asking if, at very short notice, I could attend a small-breed show and run a fun agility training ring as a friend who had committed to do it had fallen ill. It was short notice and a hassle to transport my equipment, but I agreed to help her out.

I arrived early in the morning at the show with a trailer full of equipment and started to set up a short, easy course before everyone else began to arrive. When I'd finished setting up I had time to kill before the event started. It was a sunny but cool February day, and I decided to wander around to the far side of the field and get a cup of tea to warm my hands.

And then it happened. I saw her. My heart skipped a beat as I saw the most beautiful pup I'd ever seen. The most amazing and life-changing dog I have ever known, and probably will ever know, was just about to enter my life.

At the edge of the field there was a mesh dog run with a large, spacious kennel in it. In the run was one very fluffy Border Collie puppy who was sitting watching the comings and goings of the arriving vehicles and people. She was densely coated, beautifully marked, a very strange colour – one I'd never seen before, and she immediately caught my eye. Behind her in the kennel I saw a large dog bed and in it, three other puppies piled on top of one another, one a familiar black and white, another a more rare red and white, and the third an even rarer blue and white. All three were sleeping in a multi-coloured puppy pile. How lovely and how unusual they looked!

But the funniest-coloured one of all was alone in the run, seemingly fascinated by the passing vehicles. As I wandered over to take a closer look, the strangely coloured pup completely ignored me. A few moments later and a lady appeared asking me if I liked the pup. I certainly did, who wouldn't! Was I looking for a Border Collie, she enquired? As it happens, I was! She told me that the pups were just six weeks old that day and that sadly there was only one left. A bitch. "This bitch." She pointed at the funny-coloured pup I so admired. Could it be possible that this gorgeous pup was soon to be mine?

She let me into the pen so I could pick up the pup. The noise awoke the other puppies and they came out sleepily, wagging their tails and asking for my attention, seemingly desperate to be picked up. But the pup that interested me didn't want to be picked up and as I held her, she looked away from me and scrabbled frantically to be let loose, her sharp little claws scraping at my neck. She was still focused on the passing traffic and in that behaviour I should have seen a clue as to what I was letting myself in for. But my instant attraction overrode my usual observations, and subject to my meeting both her parents and seeing her health tests, I agreed that I would surely buy this beautiful, characterful, unusual pup that smelt of sweet biscuits, as healthy puppies do.

It seems incredible to me now, as it did then, that this had happened so very soon after I had declared my wishes. When I first saw her, I had doubted she would be for sale. Surely no one would want to sell such an unusual and striking-looking animal? But she was the only one left for sale. How strange. I wondered vaguely why she was left when she was so unusual, but I failed to ask and the deed was done; I had my very first puppy.

When my boyfriend saw her, he stated confidently and with a wry smile, "Looks like you found exactly what you are looking for. It's just meant to be!"

One week later, Cloud was to come to live with me. I couldn't sleep, I was so excited and I spent the week dashing round puppy-proofing the house and garden and buying puppy things in an excited frenzy.

★

The day soon dawned and with it feelings of excitement, but also trepidation. A new puppy was a huge commitment, even for an experienced dog owner and trainer. I asked a friend to journey with me as I had to take the other dogs and I wanted Cloud to have someone to hold and comfort her on the car journey home. I'd heard so many tales of puppies being sick, having diarrhoea and panicking during their first car journey. I wanted someone kind and knowledgeable to comfort her, should she be frightened. Additionally, I didn't really know how well Cassie and Lace would cope with a pup. Lace I knew would not like her. She hated puppies. So it was important Cloud was kept safe in the front seat until I was in a position to manage the introductions at home.

Equipped with baby wipes, towels and a water bowl, my friend was well prepared to hold the puppy on the hour-long journey home. Off we set to pick up Cloud.

The moment I had her in my arms again I realised that she was not like any other puppy I had met and trained at class. She clawed and scrabbled away from me. She didn't want picking up and cuddling. I installed her on my friend's lap once in the car and in that moment the education for me and for my friend began. Cloud didn't want to be held in place on the front seat, she wanted to be in the back with the two other dogs. She clawed and scrabbled at my friend's chest from the moment she got in the car, trying to climb over her shoulder, seemingly desperate to get to the two now growling and snarling dogs who had read her intent. My friend struggled as Cloud clawed and screamed her frustration at not being able to do as she pleased.

I began to wonder what I had let myself in for and for most of the next ten years I kept wondering, as Cloud brought ongoing havoc into my life. Happily, she did soften somewhat and eventually become my very best friend, my protector, my teacher, the leader of a number of dog groups and the most amazing dog I have ever known.

By the time we reached my home, my poor friend was bleeding and desperate to get away from the cute but frantic pup. Cloud had bitten her and scratched her chest and neck. I relieved my friend of Cloud and carried the still scratching, complaining animal through my living room to the garden, where I placed her on the floor. I had expected her to be nervous, worried, as new puppies often are when encountering new places. But instead, as soon as Cloud's paws hit the ground, she had a big shake, and then with her white-tipped tail arched over her back she trotted off confidently. Immediately she began to ascend the steps that led to the furthest reaches of the garden. I didn't want her climbing steps so I went to pick her up and she whirled round at me, showing her displeasure.

★

And so life with Cloud had begun. The first few months were just horrible. Cloud refused to be held or handled. She had zero interest in me unless I offered her food or play and she took very little notice of the other two dogs when they too tried to teach her dog rules, boundaries or manners.

Cassie, too old to cope with such a challenging pup, resorted to hiding away at times and I to protecting her. Lace did the best she could and eventually managed to find a technique of squashing Cloud flat on the ground, to contain her when she had her wildest moments. Cloud was like no other pup I, my other dogs, or my team of instructors had ever encountered and she had us all beat as to what to do with some of her more difficult behaviours.

But even with all that, I still loved her. In fact I adored her and deep down although her challenges worried me, I admired her sheer bloody-minded tenacity and I realised quickly that I had, in fact, been given exactly the strong-willed, educational dog I had wished for. "Be careful what you wish for," my boyfriend giggled so often, as he watched my daily struggles with her.

From very early on, some Border Collies show interest in sheep or other moving things and Cloud was no exception. It was clear that Cloud had a very high prey drive and I quickly realised that she was obsessed by, and wished to control movement of, a number of different things. Whereas my previous dogs had only really shown interest in a few things, Cloud predated on most things that moved, as well as some that didn't!

The many targets for her attention included cats, sheep, squirrels, rabbits, birds, cars, buses, joggers, skateboarders, lorries, cows, horses, deer, pigs, the local farmyard bull, pheasants, mice, rats, ducks, and most surprisingly of all to me, fish. Throughout her life, until she became too ill to do so, she often caught and ate fish from rivers, lakes and streams. It was just one of the many things she did that I have never seen my other dogs do. All through her life I had to manage her around moving targets and though I did gain some control when I trained her as a sheepdog, it was still an ongoing battle.

She was like no other dog I had ever trained before, or have since. It was like she was part wild feral animal, part pet.

Curiously, she had no interest whatsoever in tractors or chickens! And though most animals on the planet were potential prey, she would run happily through a flock of clucking, flapping chickens without batting an eyelid. Cloud was the strongest, most determined, most 'abnormal' dog I have ever known.

But it wasn't until Cloud was tall enough to see out of the car window that I realised I had a very real and immediate problem on my hands. She decided that when in the car, she must fixate through the front window at oncoming vehicles, and as they passed us, heading in the opposite direction, she must chase them and then bite the window when she could chase them no further. To this day the car that Cloud 'grew up in' has a scratch in the glass from one of her attacks, an attack that knocked out one of her own teeth!

As she fixated and whirled, she drooled continuously so that when she whirled round in pursuit of a car, a long stream of drool whizzed around, splattering me, passengers, the other dogs, the windows and the furnishings. Few people wanted to travel with me.

Realising this was neither safe nor pleasant, I tried all I could to halt her seemingly tireless pursuit of cars. First I tried a car harness. But her launches, halted by the harness, resulted in her damaging her own shoulder and laming herself very badly. I tried a different harness, but she just chewed through it. So then I decided to cage her. She still whirled in her cage and bit at the bars and on one occasion hit the back wall of the cage so hard she nearly upended it. So then I covered the cage, hoping that not seeing the cars would reduce her enthusiasm. But then she simply followed the sound of cars and added barking in frustration to the existing behaviour problem.

Whenever possible, I had a friend travel with us and hold her on a lead in the very centre of the car so she couldn't damage herself or the car. I even tried putting her in the foot well and securing her there, but she tore at the soft seat covering with her claws and teeth, like a wild animal. Travelling became a very hazardous occupation for us all.

At home, I was routinely taking her to roads and trying and failing to counter condition her to be calm and still near traffic. One day I decided that I would sit near a road for as long as it took until she got exhausted and calmed. After eight hours I gave up and went home. She was getting worse, every day.

I took the other dogs, all well-mannered and uninterested in cars, to set an example to the still-young pup. She knocked them over in her launches and despite Lace giving her some very stern tellings-off she continued, her enthusiasm completely unabated. I tried Turn and Face, my own technique that had been so successful in halting fixations, aggression, reactivity and fear in dozens and dozens of dogs. But she battled against every attempt I made and in the end I would just sit down exhausted and give up. She knew I would. She knew that she had more energy and enthusiasm than I had. It was like she had been sent to test me, to taunt me, to teach me that I was nothing. Though it seemed ridiculous at times, I felt like she was laughing at me, as though she had been deliberately engineered and designed to prove me wrong in every one of my beliefs and to zero out every dog-training skill I had acquired. I felt that my years of dog-training and behaviour experience amounted to nothing. Zero. All my prior successes with other dogs faded into insignificance as I tried, but failed, time and time again, to come up with solutions to calm her down, and gain some kind of control. I felt completely useless.

By now I was getting desperate with the car situation and I resorted one day to the only thing I felt I had left, just sitting down and crying. I felt better afterwards, but it did little to solve the problem.

★

My concerns with the car behaviour grew and despite consulting some of my top behaviour friends, no one could see a way to stem Cloud's behaviour. With a 300-mile journey looming over me as our holiday date grew closer, I decided that if I couldn't physically restrain her, I'd just have to resort to putting even more hours of time and effort into training her to lie down in the car and staying down so she couldn't see the cars. Cloud was supremely bright and easy to train; she picked up stuff so easily. It was almost like she had understood the English language in a previous life. But understanding what I wanted of her and doing what I wanted of her were to Cloud two very different things. She learnt commands almost immediately and she was keen to learn. But getting her to respond when she didn't want to was another matter!

Eventually the day of our holiday dawned and I had no choice but to test out whether my training had paid off.

I loaded the dogs into the car and put Cloud's cage in the centre of the vehicle, strapping it down to stop it sliding or moving. From there I could see her in the cage in my rear view mirror; I could monitor her behaviour and position as I drove.

With the car loaded, the dogs installed safely, we were ready to go so I asked her to lie down, which she did instantly and I told her to stay, which she did. A good start. But confidence wasn't flowing through me; I knew this was probably a temporary success.

I got in and started the engine. She stood up. I asked her to lie down. She lay down. I asked her to stay. I set off and within five seconds she stood again. I asked her to lie down. She didn't. I repeated the command. She eventually responded and lay down. Another five seconds went by. She stood. Then the first car came our way, she whizzed around in a circle in the deliberately small cage, spraying slobber everywhere. I felt it hit my hair. She lunged at the back of the cage and bit the bars. The car had passed. I asked her to lie down, she paused. I asked her again and she did. Then she got up again two seconds later. I asked her to lie down, she refused. I pulled over and as I opened the car door to gain access to her, she lay down.

She knew exactly what I wanted. But she didn't want to do what I wanted her to do so she just didn't do it, as was Cloud's way. We had gone less than a quarter of a mile and with another 299.75 miles of our journey still left to go, I knew this was going to be one of the longest and most testing days I had ever had. *Perhaps I should just abandon the holiday*, I wondered briefly.

And so it continued, for mile after mile, hour after hour.

Once on the motorway things were a bit easier. Although she kept disregarding my request to lie down, or repeatedly lay down and stood up again, she wasn't spinning and frantic and biting the bars as the cars which came towards us were some metres away on the other side of the crash barrier. At that distance, they didn't generate in her the need to bite the cage so we had a brief respite. But all too soon we were back on less major roads and the lie down, stand up, spin, bite, lie down, stand up, spin, bite behaviour recommenced.

One of the many things that Cloud did, that I have never seen any other dog do, was use mirrors to make eye contact. From her position in the cage, she would look deep into my eyes using my rear view mirror. Every time I asked her to lie down she would stare straight into my eyes, with her powerful, often unnerving, piercing amber eyes. She would seemingly bore into my soul, seeking out my weakness and fragility so that she could exploit it.

In her, I had 'met my match', my friends would say.

I was becoming very tired and my determination was dissolving through mental exhaustion. The battle of wills continued unabated for many more very long miles, before finally, after over 200 miles and four hours of continuous lying down and standing up, I could persist no more. I was exhausted, defeated, deflated and holding back desperate tears of frustration.

During my holiday I would try to come up with a better, more cunning plan for the journey home. Though what that plan might be, I had no idea.

And so it was that I decided that if she wouldn't stay lying down then at least I could pretend that I had 'won' by instructing her to not lie down, by going along with what she had wanted all along. But at least this way it would be under my request, not hers. As we stopped at some traffic lights in a lovely little Welsh town, I asked her again to lie down. She looked at me in the mirror and once more regarded me for a second or two, before lying down. And then as soon as she lay, I executed my most cunning plan. The only thing I could think of to save face.

I asked her to stand.

"Cloud – stand!" I said in a cheery voice which belied my inner weakness. She stood, instantly.

Then with a long, hard stare into my eyes through the rear view mirror, as if trying to work out how she herself could win this battle, then as if she was surprised at my stupidity, as if she was shocked that I could be so dumb, she seemed to arrive at some conclusion of her own.

Once again, disregarding my command, she circled slowly. No doubt also exhausted, she sighed a big, weary sigh, then she lay down, curled up and went to sleep!

She didn't move again until we arrived at our destination.

I'm still not entirely sure which of us won this particular battle, but I had learned a great lesson. If you want Cloud to do something that she doesn't want to do, ask her to do the opposite. And by deliberately disregarding my request, she would in fact conform to my wishes.

Yayyyyy! Success. Sort of.

Cloud was a born leader. She was the greatest lesson of my life. Her strength and courage inspired so many. Her power influenced so much and her amazing ability with other dogs saved many lives.

★

To my amazing girl Cloud, I miss you so much; it hurts me, every day. When I think of you and write of you, I cry in pain. I hope that you forgive my mistakes, that you forgive my not being able to mend your broken body, and that you know I will hold you in my heart for all time, until one day we may meet again.

Whereupon you can once again disregard my commands. And in so doing, I know that all is as it should be. That the universe is unfolding, exactly as it should!

Run free, Cloud. Run long and stay strong, as I know you surely will.

Ode to Cloud

If it wasn't for the dog, there would be a lot less mess
If it wasn't for the dog, there would be a lot less stress
If it wasn't for the dog, my dinner would have no hair
If it wasn't for the dog there'd be no tennis ball on the
stair.

If it wasn't for the dog, I'd not be walking in the rain
If it wasn't for the dog, each day might be the same
If it wasn't for the dog, my health would be much worse
If it wasn't for the dog I'd be under a very lonely curse.

If it wasn't for the dog, my house would be less smelly
If it wasn't for the dog, I might never wear my wellies
If it wasn't for the dog, I'd have a lot less sleepless nights
If it wasn't for the dog there'd be a lot less online fights.

If it wasn't for the dog, I'd have the sofa to myself
If it wasn't for the dog, there'd be no trophies on the
shelf
If it wasn't for the dog, I'd not have met the friends I did
If it wasn't for the dog, some days in bed I would have
hid.

If it wasn't for the dog, there wouldn't have been all
those smiles
If it wasn't for the dog, I'd not have walked those endless
miles
If it wasn't for the dog, I'd rarely see the starry sky
And if it wasn't for the dog, good times would pass me
by.

If it wasn't for the dog, there'd be no greeting at the
door
If it wasn't for the dog, there'd be no paw prints on the
floor
If it wasn't for the dog, I could sleep away the day
If it wasn't for the dog, with whom now would I play?

If it wasn't for the dog, I'd spend less time sweeping hair
If it wasn't for the dog, my bank account would be less
bare
If it wasn't for the dog, there'd not be places that I went
I think to keep me active, this dog was surely sent.

If it wasn't for the dog, I'm not sure what I'd do
If it wasn't for the dog, I know I'd feel more blue
If it wasn't for the dog, I'd feel sad and so alone
Over mountains, hills and valley, I'm not sure that I'd
have roamed.

And if it wasn't for the dog, I'd not be parked outside
the vet's
If it wasn't for the dog, I'd not be awaiting results of
tests
If it wasn't for the dog, I'd not be feeling sad today
If only the vet would tell me, that my fears could go
away.

If it wasn't for the dog, I'd not be sat here now and
crying
When I look now at my dog, I know that she is dying
If it wasn't for the dog, I'd not have to make this choice
If only she could speak to me, I wish she had a voice.

And now my dog has gone away, to where I do not know
I sit alone and think of her, I feel so very low.
But I know one day the pain will leave, my broken
shattered heart
And I can look back and remember her, so we will never
be apart.

Why do we get a dog, when we know the pain they
cause?
Why do we want our kitchen floor covered in muddy
paws?
Why do we suffer with them, when we could choose to
be alone?
Maybe it's because without a dog, there really is no
home?

When they up and go and leave us, crying on the floor
When there's no more wagging tail to greet us at the
door
When there's no barking in our ear, no licking of our
face
We know we have arrived at an empty, lonely place.

Now please if you'll excuse me, I have something now
to do
I know I'll suffer once again, if choose this plan I do.
But I have to find another way, to stop me feeling blue
I'm off to get another dog – what else am I to do?

Fritz:
The Dog Who Lost His Sit

It seems a strange and curious thing to me how sometimes it is so hard to see something until something or someone switches the lights on. This was one of the most illuminating cases I have ever done, and when I look back now, it is hard to imagine how I had never previously come to see the things that I learnt from it.

At the time this case came in I had already been teaching dog classes and doing behaviour work for several years and had seen thousands of dogs. But it took a very special dog and owner to make me think more deeply, and start to 'see' things in new ways.

This is the case of a dog called Fritz.

Fritz's owner rang to tell me his problem. He was an experienced dog owner and had been competing in obedience for a few years with Fritz, his youngest dog. Fritz was a three-year-old Belgian Shepherd who loved doing obedience, had progressed well and had recently qualified for the final of a major competition which was due to take place in a few weeks. The problem with Fritz, he told me, with some embarrassment in his voice, was that in the last few weeks he had refused to sit when directly in front of his owner. Although Fritz was competing at the highest levels of obedience, he had suddenly

184

and for no apparent reason decided that he was just no longer willing to sit, on his owner's request.

"I just can't figure it out," his owner told me. "One day everything was fine, and then the next day, he just refused to sit and since then he just won't do it. Well, he will do it if he isn't near and in front of me, but if he is near me, he won't. He still sits when at heel, and he will still sit when he is doing distance control. But if he is close to the front of me then he just won't do it. He won't sit at the end of his recall and we have this final coming up in just three weeks. I need to fix it and I need to fix it quickly, otherwise I can't go to the final. Someone suggested you might be able to help. Do you think that you can?"

The present position in UK competition obedience requires that the dog sit directly in front of the handler. In modern UK obedience, at the highest levels, this often requires that the dog be very close to the handler in this position, even leaning up against the handler's legs and looking directly up at them. It is a physically demanding position for the dog, so my immediate thought was *pain*. Probably his neck, or maybe his back or hips.

"Have you seen a vet?" I enquired.

As if reading my mind exactly as my thoughts presented themselves, he replied, "Oh yes, he has had X-rays and scans. At first I thought it might be pain in his hips or his back or neck and so did my vet, but nothing has been found on the scans or X-rays. In fact, the vet said he has rarely seen such a good skeletal structure in a dog. He has regular physiotherapy and the physio nurse can find nothing wrong with him either. I don't understand why he sits at heel and at a distance but not when he is close to me. It's not his hips, back or neck, so what can it be? My current trainer can see nothing wrong and neither can my friends. What do you think it could be? Can I bring him to see you?"

I love a challenge and so I was very much looking forward to seeing this strange mystery of a case, so I booked him in and then spent the next few days thinking over possibilities. I even had a dream about the problem but the dream made no sense and didn't help me. Try as I might I couldn't come up with anything other than it must be pain.

Fritz arrived at my training venue and the moment I clapped eyes on him I fell in love with the dog, and with the relationship that dog and owner shared. Fritz only had eyes for his owner. He glanced at me and acknowledged my presence but the whole time they were there, Fritz only really had eyes for his owner.

Fritz moved freely and with power and strength. He looked well, had a glossy well-brushed coat and his bright eyes shone with intelligence. His owner glowed with pride when I complimented him as we stood and chatted. Fritz looked up adoringly at his owner as he stood calmly at his side.

We talked through the details and then I asked to see Fritz in motion and performing the sits he was willing to make. I asked to see his heelwork. With a seemingly invisible request the man asked Fritz into the competition heel position. Fritz sprang into position, aligned himself perfectly at his owner's side, and sat. They stepped off together like they were one, in normal pace forward, and he then went round the room doing complex left-hand turns, about turns, left-about turns, changes of pace, and halts. Fritz was clearly enjoying the process very much and it was a joy to watch dog and owner in perfect harmony. Fritz's tail was high and wagging and he held his attention perfectly. He seemed to mind-read his handler's imminent positional changes and I held my breath at the sheer beauty of the harmony and joy of their relationship. He moved off again in fast pace, then slow pace. When the man halted, Fritz immediately dropped into a perfect sit, in good position and seemingly with no pain evident. Maybe it wasn't pain, then?

I asked him to walk and trot Fritz up and down in front of me on a relaxed lead so that I could see his natural movement. Fritz moved with such elegance. He had a straight, flowing, natural high step, born of power, balance and poise. He was a great-looking animal and seemed to thoroughly enjoy every action his owner asked of him. It was so beautiful to watch, and for a moment I forgot what I was there to do as I revelled in seeing such harmony, such synchronicity, such connection, between a dog and its owner.

Remembering my purpose, I then asked him to show me his distance control. Distance control in UK obedience requires that the dog move between the positions of sit, stand and down, in any order, several times, at a distance many metres from its owner and without tracking forward or backward too much. It's a complex task to teach well, but is a joy to watch a keen dog do.

From the other side of the room, he asked Fritz to go into sit from the down position he had left him in. Fritz bounced up into sit. He asked for a down and Fritz hit the deck instantly, before his owner even finished saying the word. He asked again for a sit; Fritz sprang seemingly without effort into a perfect sit. He asked for stand; the dog stood. Then he repeated the commands, and so it went on until I called a halt to it. The dog's responses were immediate and enthusiastic and he looked as if he was really enjoying it. What could possibly be wrong to cause him to not sit when close to his handler's front?

With Fritz now back near him, the time had come to see the problem.

Fritz stood on a loose lead in front of his owner, looking up at him and awaiting his request keenly. His tail was wagging and he was totally engaged.

"Okay, please ask him to sit." I held my breath.

"Fritz, sit."

Suddenly Fritz's whole demeanour changed for just a second: his ears flicked back momentarily and he took two steps backward away from his owner. He didn't sit. Then he yawned. Something had upset Fritz.

I asked the man to perform a formal recall so that I could see Fritz's formal present, where he needed to sit directly in front of his handler. He set Fritz up for the recall with him at his side, before leaving his side and moving several paces in front of the dog. He halted, turned to face Fritz and then he called him. Fritz set off quickly toward his owner, but then slowed; his tail showed signs of drooping and his ears had flicked back again, signalling concern. As he arrived in front of his owner, he halted a metre away and just stood there. He looked worried.

How very strange.

"What do you think is wrong?" his owner asked me. I had absolutely no idea.

Fritz was clearly anxious about sitting in front of his owner. What could possibly be upsetting him so? Had his owner punished the dog for his failure to sit, I wondered?

"When he first started doing this, did you get cross with him?" I enquired.

"Oh gosh, no! Fritz has always been so keen to please me, I adore him, my first thought was that something was wrong with him, so no, I didn't get cross. I just tried a few times, it didn't work, so I went off to ask my trainer, then my friends and then my vet. No one could see what was wrong – they were all mystified."

I was mystified too. Time for more digging.

At times like this I often find that handling a dog to see what it does with me helps. That way I can work out if the error is something the owner is doing or something inherent in the dog. I asked if Fritz would work with me and the man suggested that that was Fritz's choice, and to ask the dog. I took Fritz by his lead and asked for him to come to my side into heel. He stared at me blankly for a moment, before returning his attention to his owner and disregarding me totally. I went to my liver cake bag, and placing food in my left hand, I tried again. That worked! Fritz came uncertainly to my side in an effort to get to the liver cake. I gave him some, but retained some in my hand. I moved off with Fritz at my side and he went with me, keen for more liver cake. He looked up attentively as he flowed at my side and I felt that amazing thing that I had felt with my own dogs in this position. As I moved left and right, Fritz moved smoothly with me. I halted abruptly and Fritz behaved as the impeccably trained dog he was and sat immediately at my side. I praised him, gave him the cake, and then he immediately broke position and pulled back to his owner. His attention on me had only been temporarily created by the food. Gosh, how I loved this dog and his owner!

With Fritz now back with his owner, I was still none the wiser, so as thinking had failed I decided to just stare at the dog in case I could 'see' something. But the more I looked, the more I saw nothing.

Now it was time for another test. Fritz had sat at my side happily enough during heelwork, but would he sit in front of me?

I grabbed more liver cake and Fritz immediately came to me. He stood in front of me. Using standard methods to lure a dog into sit, I raised the food slightly above his head and asked for sit. He sat immediately in front of me and I smiled at him, praised him, "Good boy!" and rewarded him for it. I looked at the owner briefly and saw he looked somewhat pleased, but still confused, as was I.

I repeated it. He sat each time without any concern or without any ear flicking or yawning. The mystery was deepening. I put down the cake to see if he would sit for me without the lure. As soon as the cake was gone from my hand, the dog was also gone. He went back to his owner, so I couldn't try that.

Now that Fritz had successfully sat in front of me, I wondered somewhat desperately if that might trigger him back into sitting in front of his owner. I asked the man to request sit. Fritz backed away and looked worried again. What the heck was going on here?

So I asked the man to try with the liver cake. It had worked for me, maybe it would for him?

"Try the cake," I urged him. "Lure him into it just like I did."

Fritz looked up at the cake as the man lured and commanded a sit; there was a moment of confusion that crossed his face and then he sat. The owner beamed and praised the dog with much enthusiasm before giving him the cake. We repeated it and Fritz's confidence seemed to return. The lured sits soon came quickly, one after the next, without any look of concern. Whatever had worried Fritz before was leaving him now. Fritz's confidence had completely returned and he was sitting immediately on request again, with the assistance of the food.

I asked him to try the sit again, without the food. But Fritz's concern returned, he backed away again and failed to sit.

Fritz's owner was looking perplexed. "I can't use food in competition. What am I going to do?"

What to do? What to do?

More digging. "Think back to the very first day that this happened. Was anything different that day to your normal training sessions?" I enquired.

The owner stood and thought, trying to remember, and then he relayed his memory to me. "It was such a happy day. A really happy day: I had just had a promotion at work, and when I arrived home to tell my wife, she then told me she had just discovered that she was pregnant. I was utterly elated. We both were." I wondered briefly if the wife's pregnancy had caused the sit failures, but then I dismissed it.

He continued, still smiling, "I was so very happy, we had been trying for a baby for years and then suddenly our dreams had come true. I had to go to training that night and there I was practising 'present' as Fritz had recently started to sit a bit wonky off to the left. My instructor had helped me straighten that out and after a few little changes of my leg position, Fritz had finally got a good straight sit back and I was so happy." He smiled at the memory. "It was great, and then immediately after one straight sit, Fritz wouldn't sit again in the present position at all. But he still sat during distance control, as you have seen. That is partly why I wondered if it was pain. I thought that is why Fritz had sat wonky, maybe he was avoiding some pain and I'd made him sit straight and that had caused him pain?" The thought that he had caused Fritz pain made his face cloud over. "That's why I took him to the vet's and asked him to X-ray and scan his back, hips and neck. I took him to the osteopath too. I don't want to be hurting Fritz, he is such a great dog."

He smiled at Fritz but then looked perplexed again, before continuing, "What can be causing this?" Sadness was in his voice. Something was wrong but neither he nor I knew what. I was still baffled.

I had seen many cases before where an owner's negative emotional state or energy field had affected a dog's behaviour, but I couldn't recall having seen a situation where an owner's positive emotional state had affected a dog's behaviour for the worse. A thought popped into my head. I wondered if I could transport Fritz and his owner back in time to the moment his first failed sit had occurred. I was clutching at straws but it was all I could think of. Maybe there was something about that particular day that held the answer? The start of any behavioural problem is usually where all the important information lies.

Okay, time for a little reminiscing training. I figured if I could transport Fritz and his owner back to that day, to that last successful sit in front, and try to get him to feel the way he did that day, then maybe we could understand something more. I was getting very desperate, but more determined each moment to discover what was wrong with Fritz's sit.

I had recently begun doing meditation on a regular basis as well as some basic self-hypnosis training, so I used the skills I had learnt on Fritz's owner. I needed to recreate the positive feelings he had felt that day and get rid of the negative worry about Fritz. First I congratulated him on his forthcoming baby and the pay rise. It brought his mind away from the worry of Fritz and into a future of joy. He smiled at the thoughts.

"What do you want? A girl or a boy?" I enquired.

"Oh, I don't mind." He smiled again before whispering, "But I think secretly I want a girl; my wife wants a boy." He spoke as if the unborn baby might hear him if he said it too loud. I had successfully got him to now see his future in his mind. He would be seeing a baby girl or the joy of his wife if it was a baby boy. He looked reflective. But he was smiling, either way.

I told him that I wanted to try to create the happy feelings of that day to see if Fritz changed his behaviour in any way. I told him I'd recently learned some methods of mind focus that might help us and asked if he was willing to give it a go. He looked at me as though I was a bit weird and then agreed to my request. "Okay, try it," he said. I liked this guy: he was willing to do anything it seemed to understand his dog better.

FRITZ: THE DOG WHO LOST HIS SIT

I then began to instruct him exactly what to think and feel. "Stand with your back against this wall and lean slightly on it." He moved backwards to the wall. He was following my requests. Once a person starts to follow your request then you can ask them for more and more. It is standard salesman technique. "Now, relax and take some deep breaths. Concentrate on your breathing. Breathe in... then out... Feel the air going into you as you breathe deeply. Feel the air going in, then out. Pause at the end of your in-breath and feel your body be refreshed by that air. Now think back to that wonderful day: your wife has just announced her pregnancy." A big smile crept across his face. "You have just been given a pay rise, perfect timing for the new baby! Such a wonderful day!" His smile broadened further.

I continued to ask him to breathe deeply and slowly, and I talked of all the joy the new baby might bring. I asked him to remember the very moment that his wife had announced the joyous news, how he felt. Then I asked him to feel how he felt when he realised that the recent pay rise would help with the baby. Such perfect timing. Then if he could imagine his baby daughter starting to toddle about as she grew bigger, and to imagine the look on her face on her first Christmas morning. Could he see the pure wonder and joy in her eyes, on her face, as she saw the twinkling lights on her very first Christmas tree and the glossy presents underneath? As he continued to breathe and to *feel* the feelings he had that were associated with happy past and future events, he went deeper into the happy feelings. "Keep breathing," I told him, "deep and slow. Just breathe and feel the feelings of those happy days."

I then talked some more of the happy pay rise day, the first day knowing they were to have a baby, that happy, happy day, before Fritz's sit had failed.

Then I asked him to close his eyes, and once he had, I quietly reached for some liver cake and without his owner knowing, I lured Fritz in close in front of his owner and into the sit position. Fritz sat obligingly, without concern. I silently gave Fritz the cake as a reward and hoped he would retain the sit position in front of his owner.

I continued to instruct Fritz's owner. "Such happiness can bring you great strength. I bet you can now control Fritz just with your mind, you won't need words anymore. Try it *now*, in your mind, command Fritz to sit. Do it, *now*!"

I watched as he squeezed his lips together hard in concentration, his closed eyes and whole face crunched up with the effort, as he willed Fritz to sit with his mind.

"Now open your eyes," I said.

As he opened his eyes, there was Fritz, sitting right in front of him!

His face broke into a look of ecstasy and in the rapture of all the positive feelings he had just had, coupled with seeing Fritz sitting there in front of him after the failures of the last few weeks, he almost exploded with joy, and with a cry of "Good boy, Fritz!" he suddenly lunged forward toward his dog with both hands and went to ruffle his ears and the sides of his face in glee.

It caught Fritz by surprise and as soon as he made contact with Fritz's face, the dog's response was immediate and brought all the clarity we needed. He recoiled from the man's touch, stepped back, and with his ears pinned back, he shifted uncomfortably on his front legs and he looked worried again. For a few moments I saw his left eye repeatedly blink shut, and his mouth opened and shut a few times, in pain, as he paddled his front legs on the floor.

A moment of realisation hit the owner and me at the same time: he had hurt Fritz with his hands. *Something was wrong with Fritz!* His face changed from ecstasy to sadness and horror. "There must be something wrong with Fritz. Poor boy." Tears welled up in his eyes. "My poor boy," he repeated.

But we had our answer, or at least we were a lot closer to the answer. On that day, the day of great elation, when the baby was announced and the pay rise had come and Fritz had sat straight after a period of sitting wonky, his owner had been so happy that he had done something he didn't normally do. He had literally been bursting with joy and had reached out and ruffled Fritz's face and ears in an effort to show his dog how pleased he was with him and to express his joy. And in so doing, he had hurt Fritz, but hadn't realised it.

After more discussion we decided that Fritz must have some pain in his head or ears and he was taken back to the vet. The owner had originally been so sure that there was pain in his back, hips or neck that he had instructed the vet specifically to look for that. Neither he nor the vet had thought to look too deeply at any other area. An easy oversight to make when the symptoms of the behaviour did indeed indicate problems in those areas. The confusion had been caused by the fact that Fritz wasn't hurt by the actual sit movement, but instead by the *consequence of the sit* – the head ruffle on that particular day when the owner had behaved differently because of his elated emotional state. The consequence of the sit was something that the vet would never have been able to see, and something that the owner had forgotten which was only related to that specific day. But Fritz had remembered it. An intelligent, sensitive dog, Fritz had decided to avoid incurring any more pain by refusing to sit when he was in front of his owner, in case the owner once again rubbed his sore area.

The owner was so worried for Fritz but so thankful to me for what I had helped him to learn. "I must go straight back to the vet," he concluded. "Thank you so much."

As he went to leave, he paused and looked at me for a moment with a look I could not quite describe, before asking me a question. "So, can I really use my mind to command Fritz to sit now, after you did all that witchy mind stuff?"

It was a genuine enquiry and one I didn't really have an answer for. He may have been able to. But I owned up to what I had done – luring Fritz into a sit. I confessed all. He smiled at me with devilment in his eyes. He knew he had just been 'had'.

But I told him to try it anyway. "Why not, you never know!" I said. Because you never do know for sure, unless you try something. I do believe some people, with some animals, do seem to have some kind of psychic connection. But whether that connection can extend to manifesting a straight present sit, I am not sure.

★

Fritz was taken back to the vet and after an examination centred on his mouth, ears and face, was found to have a swelling above one of his very back teeth which had a small, vertical crack in it, and this had caused a low-grade infection. Treatment was given, the tooth was removed, and with a little bit of retraining, first with food and later without, Fritz's perfect sit returned.

I don't actually know if Fritz won the competition they had been training so hard for, but I certainly think that both he and his owner deserved to!

Whoever would have thought that a dog might not sit because he had a sore mouth? Fact sometimes really is stranger than fiction.

When the Student Is Ready, the Teacher Will Appear

Fritz's case didn't end there. It had set me thinking... I had seen other dogs whose 'sit' had intermittently failed and I wondered if this was a more common thing than I had previously realised.

The following week when I returned to teach my classes a truly astonishing thing happened. Although I had already taught thousands of dogs and owners over many years, for the first time I could now see something that I had never seen before. Fritz's case had opened my eyes to a whole new possibility.

We all have belief systems – things that we think are facts, things we have heard, been told, or read. We adopt them as facts as we have no knowledge to counteract them, but in reality they are just other people's views or our own ill-informed beliefs. Belief systems are in fact temporary states of thinking that are apt to change when they are confronted with actual personal experience or greater understanding. Fritz had proven a point of great noteworthiness. It had been extreme, and medical in nature, but still it made him an 'outlier' very worthy of further consideration. The secret to understanding the potential range of behaviours in any species is to look at the outliers, in this case those dogs that have extreme forms of behaviour or condition. Those dogs are the ones that show us just what dogs are truly capable of, not what we might consider the range of 'normal or common behaviour'.

As I looked more closely at the behaviour of puppies and dogs in my classes, I was stunned to see that in most cases with class dogs, when an owner touched their dog's head or ruffled its ears as part of their 'praise ritual', the dog withdrew its head somewhat or completely. They didn't often break the sit position, though a few did. It wasn't because they had bad teeth or were in pain like Fritz, it was because they just didn't like it. Mostly they tolerated it, but few seemed to actually see this type of reward as rewarding! All those years and all those dogs, we had been training dogs to sit and do other things by effectively punishing them with an ear/head ruffle and then rewarding them with liver cake. They had put up with the ear ruffle to gain the liver cake. We had actually been punishing the correct behaviour all this time and still getting quite good results.

I was astonished to concede that I had never realised or been able to see this before. Fritz's case had brought me a new thought process and from that moment forward I could suddenly see something new. That part of my former belief system was now gone and I could see something clearly. Everywhere I looked in training classes it seemed, dogs were recoiling from their owners' touch.

Many dogs like affection and touch from their owners. But some do not. Some like their head being touched or their ears being ruffled, but most it seemed, in class, would much prefer a smile or a thumbs-up sign, a clicker marker, or just verbal praise with a happy voice, followed by delivery of the food, if you are using food. To this day, I remain astonished that it took a case such as Fritz's for me to realise this.

Over the many years of classes since this realisation has occurred, I have noticed more and more how humans seem to have an inbuilt desire to touch their dogs as a consequence to them having performed a correct action, or as a sign of affection.

But *how* you touch a dog and where and when you touch it is key here. Many owners ruffle their dog's ears vigorously. It can't be nice – how would you feel if I ruffled your ears? Or rubbed your face vigorously or patted you on the head?

An ear massage is one thing; controlled, with the dog being able to move away if it chooses, performed in a gentle and soothing way, but the ruffling that many owners do can't be pleasant and with such delicate hearing, must also be quite loud for most dogs!

Likewise a pat on the head or a vigorous rub of the head area must be for some most unpleasant. Likewise a firm pat on the ribs! We can ask ourselves, *who* is it rewarding for, us – or them?

We know that when a human touches a furred animal it loves then the human's blood pressure and heart rate can be lowered. A beneficial biological reward for the human. But is it the case that this benefits dogs also?

Since this realisation I have now banned the rubbing of a dog's head or ears as a reward in my classes. And in so doing we have seen improved responses to all aspects of training. We talk about this phenomenon in our introduction night before all our new courses commence. To demonstrate the point I ask owners to place their hands over their own ears and then rub them vigorously whilst saying "good boy". Try it now, yourself. Then I ask them to say "good boy" as they hit themselves on the head or bang their hand onto their own ribcage and say "good girl". A look of enlightenment drifts over each person's face when they do this to themselves. They realise that in most cases and for most people and dogs, it is not a pleasant experience. But it is one which for most humans appears to be an ingrained desire.

Furthermore, I have come to the conclusion that in fact there is a large percentage of dogs *who don't like physical contact at all* with their owners. And there are many more who do not like physical contact with other people.

I have owned two such dogs myself: Cloud and Connor. Both Cloud and Connor have never wanted to be touched. Cloud had no time for affection (except on the day she was dying – on that day she screamed if I removed my hand from touching her) though she would occasionally tolerate a formal massage, as will Connor. But both Cloud and Connor (both working breeds, high-drive dogs in different ways) would sooner 'work' then have touch. Connor and Cloud would both withdraw from any attempt I made to stroke them, rub them or touch them. All of my others have enjoyed touch – though not all of them in the face area – and Cassie, Lace, Mirk, Karma and Cherry all sought or seek touch and will come and have a cuddle, or choose to lie on or near me or other humans. But even then, if I tried to touch their heads when they were working, they would recoil.

Over time, I learnt and had to accept that with Cloud and Connor their idea of connection with me *was for us to do something together*. They much preferred to be given a task to do – to fetch sheep, to do close heelwork, to pick up an item and bring it to me, to follow commands, to engage in a learning process, or to connect on a movement or mind basis, via obedience, tricks, agility or sheepwork. With both Cloud and Connor our relationship excelled only when we were working together, and not when we were sitting together.

Paradoxically, it has been Cloud and Connor who I have done the most public demonstrations with. On every occasion that either dog has worked publicly people have come up to me afterwards and made comments such as "She only has eyes for you", or "Wow, he was glued to your every word or movement" or similar things. On occasion judges at obedience competitions I have been in with Cloud and Connor have commented with words like, "Great attention from your dog" or "It's beautiful to see such a close bond – well done!" Yet it was these two same dogs who, at home, would avoid contact with me. The connection we shared during demonstration or periods of work was just that – a connection based on *doing something together.* Working-bred Border Collies have been bred to work with a human. That is their breed purpose, so it is unsurprising therefore that some of them and two of mine excelled in having a connection only when they were working with me. If you think about it, many humans have this with some of their friends too. I have had friends who I rode horses with, walked with, went swimming with, or went on holiday with. I felt no need to sit and stroke any of them. I can only imagine their reaction if I suddenly tried it. Touching and stroking is something I only do with my partner.

Unlike all of my other dogs, Connor has such a strong connection with doing something with a human that he will actually go off with a complete stranger if that stranger is willing to continuously throw him a ball. He will leave me and Simon on a walk if we tire of throwing, but someone else nearby is willing. He will walk up to any and all strangers and attempt to get them to play with him. He will pick up leaves, sticks, stones, balls, even a single blade of grass and present it to a total stranger. If that stranger engages with him, as they often do, then he will continue to play with them even if Simon and I and the other dogs walk away. Though he will come if we call him, he is often reluctant to do so. To him, the benefit of having a human is purely one of 'engagement through activity', not affection. Additionally he will often tolerate a brief head touch from a stranger, but only as a way to gain their initial attention. After a few seconds he will withdraw and pick

ALL SIX LEGS

something up for them to throw for him. If they try again to touch him after engagement with an 'item' has commenced, he will dodge their touch or pull away from them.

This type of dog is not wrong, it is just different. But for an owner who has acquired a dog because they like to fuss a dog, it can be confusing and upsetting. Many people call me to tell me they need help with their dog because their dog 'dislikes' or 'hates' them. That is how I felt initially with Cloud and Connor. I thought that they disliked me.

These non-contact dogs can at times be very challenging to live with. At the end of a long and tiring day, or when I feel ill or sad, I love to sit on the sofa and have one or more of my dogs lie next to me, or with their heads on me so that I can stroke them. That is one of the main reasons I like dogs – because they feel nice to touch and watching them enjoy that touch brings me pleasure as in many cases they enjoy touch as much as I do. I like stroking my own dogs. To the dogs who like touch, *stroking is an activity*. But with Cloud and Connor at the end of a long day what they wanted was to do something else, or to rest peacefully alone somewhere. To them, stroking was not an activity but an inconvenient annoyance that gets in the way of doing 'something else'. When all I had was Cloud and Connor in my life, my 'cuddle needs' went unfulfilled and when I was worn out or ill, their 'doing something else' needs also went unmet.

After Cloud and Connor came re-homed Mirk, a love monster, then puppy Karma, a love monster in the extreme, and then Simon's dog Cherry, another loving dog. All of them would happily take affection over and above doing something else. They would snuggle me if I was ill or tired. None of the dogs were right or wrong, good or bad, just different.

In 2018 I started a couple of research threads on Facebook, asking owners whether their dogs sought affection and physical

202

contact with them. Owners of several hundred dogs replied. Although this is an informal study and has no control group, the information provided is I believe interesting in itself.

An astonishing 17.8 per cent of all dogs owned by respondents were reported to 'never seek physical contact or affection' from their owners. Whilst some loved to lie on or near their owners or would push at their owner's hand to encourage stroking or massage, many could 'take it or leave it', but 17.8 per cent never sought any physical affection from their humans. That is nearly one in five dogs that does not seek, or seem to enjoy, physical affection with its owner.

Yet nearly every owner wants to give their dog physical contact. Some owners are distraught that their dogs don't want to be touched and take it personally, as I did, when I first realised that the cute bundle of fluff that Cloud once was just didn't want me to touch her. She was all fluff and I wanted to cuddle her, stroke her, hold her and smell her puppyness, but when I tried, she recoiled at best, or at worst, she bit me (when she was a puppy). Likewise neither Cloud nor Connor liked to be brushed, ever. Yet others I had would groan and squirm in pleasure. Cherry wags her tail and gets all giddy as soon as she sees a brush come out.

In my first book, *A Dog Behaviourist's Diary*, I wrote about dogs that didn't want to be touched by strangers and that those dogs should have their personal space respected. I wrote that it is my belief that touching a dog who does not want to be stroked is a great way of provoking a dog to bite. But when you consider that nearly one in five don't even want to be touched by their own owners, then it is likely that those dogs don't want to be touched by strangers either, though a rare few do seem to prefer touch from strangers than from their owners.

With this in mind it amazes me that dogs who don't like being touched don't bite a lot more often than they do!

No dogs should be forced to have touch, if they don't like it. As no human should. We are all different. Each of us has to learn what our dogs do and do not like and we need to remember that what might be rewarding to one dog could feel horrible to another. What we want from our relationship with our own dog might be different to what our dog wants.

Each dog is unique. He or she is who they are. *Why* they are as they are remains at times unclear to me, but it appears from research or observation that those dogs who are particularly 'high drive' or focused on work can sometimes prefer to work than snuggle. Likewise it appears that commonly the most intelligent dogs seem rather more reluctant to have affection than to engage in 'brain games'. But then I can think of a few humans that are this way too! I know people whose main interest in life is to work, their human relationships with their spouse or even their children are secondary to their drive to work.

Your dog is like you, a complex and unique individual, and to get the best from him you need to understand his wishes too and make sure that your rewards are also rewarding to him! And that his needs are met.

*

I would like to thank all those people who took part in my research threads of 2018 for supplying information about their dogs' likes and dislikes.

But the biggest thanks of all goes to Fritz and his owner for bringing me new understanding, for helping me to 'see'; and in so doing helping many thousands of dogs to enjoy their training more and thousands of owners to understand their dogs better.

Thank you all.

Turn and Face Marches On

In my first book, *A Dog Behaviourist's Diary*, I shared the story of Sabre, a six-year-old German Shepherd who had been on-leash reactive to dogs since adolescence. Sabre had reacted at pretty much every dog he had seen since that time and although his owner, who was very committed to resolving his issues and a very talented owner/trainer too, had gone to great lengths to resolve his reactivity, travelling the country seeing trainer after trainer, Sabre's behaviour hadn't improved.

Live in front of an audience of budding dog-training and behaviour enthusiasts, I took Sabre and his owner through the process of understanding and using my own self-created reactivity solution, Turn and Face (now commonly known as TAF). Sabre's reactivity ceased that day, a few minutes after the application of the technique. The whole group on that course stood open-mouthed when Sabre fell silent and they marvelled at how relaxed he was as he walked up and down past seven different dogs. For me and the team at CaDeLac it was business as usual, albeit when it comes to TAF, that particular 'business' is often completely amazing to see.

We did this same thing every week and had been doing so for years. For most dogs, around nine out of ten, TAF has an immediate positive transformative effect. It is often a very extraordinary thing to see: a barking, lunging dog fall into a state of calmness and peace and then walk around or with other dogs without barking or lunging. Sadly though, for some, TAF fails completely and we have to use one of our other processes. The relationship between Sabre and his owner was a particularly good one; his respect for her meant that he quickly responded to the changes that she was asking of him, via the Turn and Face process. Sabre didn't react again to any dog that day. His reactivity faded away completely over the following few days once he was home, which was reported by his owner on an internet forum.

A week later he was off-lead walking with a group of our instructors' dogs. Three weeks later he was in a class, completely non-reactive. In the end, it turned out that Sabre was actually an incredible 'teaching dog'. What I mean by that is a dog who by its very nature (what its genes tell it to do), or sometimes its learnt behaviour (behaviour which is based on its life experiences), knows how to get other dogs to change their ways.

Some well- and appropriately socialised dogs tend to have this skill, but it would seem that there are others that just have it innately.

People are the same. Sometimes a good parent just happens to be a good parent, even if they've had no prior 'training' in the form of caring for a younger sibling, or watching others do it. They might even have had poor parenting and yet still turn into a good parent; some people are just good at it, is how it seems to me, in the same way as some people are naturally musical, or artistic, or can see how things work and can fix them. Others might be talented in the form of creating things, or be good with animals; they may have the gift of the gab, or be natural salespeople. Yet others are naturally witty, or just have a certain charisma that most can detect, but few could truly define.

Dogs are the same. They often have roles. Some are natural teachers, some are peacekeepers. Others fulfil parental roles, even if they are not themselves parents. Other still teach play, or rules, they halt over-boisterous behaviour, they reprimand youngsters for wrongdoings, and they lead by example.

Sabre, who had been reacting for nearly six years, had inside him a dog that then went on to lead group walks and fulfil an educational role in groups of dogs. His owner also went on to foster dogs and get another dog herself. Sabre was fine with all of that. Once a dog's behaviour is changed in one way, a whole load of opportunities open up for the dog and owner. New adventures to go on, more walks to be shared, new friends to be made, more joy in life.

In my previous book I explained how I had been so excited by the response of all the people who had witnessed Sabre's radical change of behaviour, I went on to an internet forum to try to share the technique with anyone who wanted to learn it. Anyone who had a reactive dog or worked with them. I wanted to share this amazing thing as far and wide as I could because I knew it could transform lives, for the dog and owner and all those who encounter the dog.

But within forty-eight hours of being on the group, I was called a liar, a fraud, a dog batterer, and a string of other uncomplimentary things by people who didn't believe, or want to believe, that reactivity can be solved quickly, kindly and effectively. I later received death threats by email; my business and my dogs' lives were threatened and I sank into a state of confused self-doubt, wondering why these people who didn't know me or my love of dogs were being so horrid. Later still, I had a brick thrown through my living room window in the middle of the night. It landed on Cassie's bed. Very fortunately, Cassie was not in it at the time. For a while I lived in fear for me and the dogs. The threats were becoming life-endangering and the police became involved. It was my first real experience of 'internet wars', or the later version, 'dog trainer wars', and it was one that haunted me. Risks to my life I could accept, but risks to my dogs' lives I could not.

So I fell silent about Turn and Face. I was too scared to share.

★

Over the following years, as I watched the dog-training world tear itself apart, I saw online battles that appeared to come from pure hatred. Terrible, awful things were said about other good trainers, and one-upmanship started to turn one trainer against another. People started to take sides and accuse others of wilful cruelty and barbarism. At the same time, I also saw what appeared to be a dramatic rise in reactivity, and the debates and fights that went with reports of such. And as I watched I realised that still, no one else seemed to be able to resolve it inside one hour. But I routinely could. The burden of this knowledge and the frustration of being unable to share it weighed heavily on my mind day and night.

Then I had a dream. I dreamt that I was witnessing a dog being put to sleep and a dog trainer standing by, telling the dog's owner, "It is the only way, he cannot be cured". I had not seen the dog react in my dream, so I had no idea whether the dog could have been 'cured' or not. But the dog died and the dream stayed with me. Just before he died, he lifted his head and looked at me, this dog I didn't know, but that was having his life terminated because no one had been able to help him, when perhaps I could have done. I tried, in the dream, to stop the process so that I could assess this dog, to see if I could help, but the needle slipped into his leg and I was powerless to stop it. The dream haunted me.

Always one to have my head in the clouds, I saw this as a sign that I must share TAF. I felt the pressure mounting on me to do it and I thought for a while that I was going mad with these thoughts, but still I was stifled by fear of the potential repercussions and I remained too scared to share.

While writing my first book, these fears still controlled me. I debated long and hard with myself and my friends as to whether it was safe to describe TAF in the book. I battled with my fears about what comeback I might have, because once it was in print, it was in print and there was no taking it back.

What if it didn't work for other people? What if someone threw another brick and it injured or killed one of my dogs? What if everyone just laughed at me and it detracted from the rest of the contents of the book? What if I was wrong? What if I couldn't explain it well enough with just words?

But what about that dog in the dream? What did it mean? What if, what if, what if? What should I do?

A wise friend listened to me one day as I battled with my inner demons and she said, "Denise, TAF has been given to you to help dogs, as you have been doing for years. What if you go to your grave knowing that you could have helped millions more dogs and their owners, if only you'd had more courage? How will you feel then?" She gave me a copy of the brilliant book *Feel the Fear and Do It Anyway*, I read it and that was it, my mind was made up. The book had informed me rightly that *courage is not the lack of fear, but is the ability to act despite the fear.* It is a brilliant book! I had a responsibility to the dogs I so admired to help as many as I could. TAF went into print and the waiting began for me. Would people like the book? Would they direct their hatred at me again? Would the book fail to sell enough copies to recover the money I had borrowed to produce and print it? Would the spiralling costs make me homeless again? Would it be my downfall? Would I be the laughing stock of the dog-training world? Was I strong enough to I survive the battering that I expected? Was I going mad with these tortuous worries and thoughts that consumed so much of each day? Would Turn and Face work for other people as it had for me? Or would it cause more trouble?

★

Within one week of the book's release a report came back via Facebook that, 'Turn and Face really works! My dog has stopped reacting. It's amazing.' For the first year I received a message nearly every day that someone's life had been transformed by TAF. They spoke of their amazement and their joy. They couldn't be more grateful to me, they said. Likewise, lovely messages came in about the book in general, and positive reviews started to appear on Amazon and on my own Facebook pages. I started to have 'Friend' requests by the dozen and I made many new acquaintances.

So with my confidence now growing I released a video clip of a TAF case on a Facebook group, and immediately several trainers contacted me wanting to know more. Trainers from all over the world. Some of them were 'big names' and had thousands of followers. The trainers who contacted me were from all sorts of different backgrounds and had many different approaches to dog training, but they all seemed to have one thing in common: many years' experience working with dogs and their reactivity issues. These experienced, wise trainers were sponges for more info about the process.

But at the same time the hate campaign was getting off the ground. I received a couple of very negative reviews about the book, and about TAF. People were raging on forums all over the world and calling me the things they had before; a liar, a dog batterer. Someone even posted that "Denise McLeod lines her pockets by killing dogs." "She breaks dogs' necks," another said. I was so sad, but it was not as bad as I had expected, so I just focused on the positive comments as best I could.

And then on New Year's Eve, four months after the book's release, the widely respected brilliant trainer and hugely experienced Martha Hoffman (director of Hearing Dog Program in the USA), who had understood and been in favour of TAF right from the start, posted on Facebook that her dog had been calmed and had gone to sleep after she had used TAF for the first time with him. He had been going berserk in their home in response to fireworks that night. *Her much-loved dog had become calm after TAF and had settled down to sleep!*

After that post, all hell broke loose. Messages on that thread and the private messages and emails that followed numbered in their thousands. While some were good trainers asking genuine questions, many were from people who had never seen TAF and were full of venom for a process that they seemingly knew nothing about. For forty-eight hours and with hardly any sleep, I responded as calmly as I could to each and every message but I was losing the battle, and the will to live. So in frustration I deleted most of my comments and most of the thread with it, and got off the internet, and went out for a long walk with the dogs. Followed by many more long walks with the dogs.

I lost many people who I had considered friends after the book came out. People who had stayed at my house, who I had visited, who I loved, left me as they fell foul of the 'Denise McLeod is a dog batterer' campaign – they didn't want the hassle of defending me. I even lost one really good friend because of the uproar the book had caused, something that saddens me deeply. But for every friend I lost I made a hundred more, some of whom have become really brilliant friends.

But still, even with evidence mounting daily in support of TAF's capacity to heal problems, I was thrown off nearly every internet forum where I tried to share the story of TAF. Groups that specialised in reactivity systematically blocked and removed me. My heart screamed at them. *Why don't you want people and their dogs to live happily and peacefully? Do you want dogs to be condemned to death even though in most cases a solution is only a few minutes away?* I genuinely did not understand these acts, and to this day it remains a mystery to me why people apparently *don't* want to help others to help their dogs.

I ran a series of TAF events and we filmed the cases live, one by one. People started to contact me to run events at their venues, and I agreed to them all. TAF was rocking and the results were great for most dogs, and I felt purposeful and full of hope. But then the people organising and promoting the events started to get battered by those that opposed TAF. They got hate mail, and someone even contacted one of the venues to tell them, "You will be killing dogs if you allow this event to continue." That event and three others were cancelled as the hosts just didn't want the hassle. An old friend wrote to me and told me that because of the uproar she had lost friends too, and she blamed and would never forgive me, she said. Another dear friend stopped supporting the book and TAF even though she herself had had success with it; even though TAF was the reason that we had become friends in the first place. She didn't need the hassle, the death threats, the condemnation of her as a trainer. I had lost a very dear friend and I was becoming lost in my own fears again.

Because of the hassle and loss of friends, twice after the release of the book I made the decision to withdraw it from sale. Twice I decided that I just couldn't carry on with the battle, the hate mail, the threats. But twice, close friends talked me out of the idea, pointing out the enormous improvements that were being made in the lives of people and dogs. And I could see for myself that it was true, that TAF continued to bring in great results: hundreds of grateful emails and messages proved it, and so I reversed my decision and plodded on.

★

But something amazing was about to happen in the form of the many trainers who were now applying their brain power to thoughts of just how useful TAF can be. With this new brain power came new thinking and new approaches too. I had used TAF mostly with dogs that react on-lead to people and other dogs; these minds that were new to TAF saw it as a process which can lower unwanted 'arousal' of any kind. Martha Hoffman (USA) had used it for calming her own sound-reactive dog with great success. She has since reported success with twenty of her cases where she has used TAF. Trish Wamsatt (USA) had some very inspired thinking and started to use it for fear of thunderstorms, with some success. Dogman Downunder (Andy Lea from Australia) started to use it in new ways, pre-training it extensively before using it live. Sharon Nelson (USA) started to use it to calm agility dogs and balance them prior to work. Gareth Rees in Wales started to use it and reported that in the space of five months, all forty-two cases had been successful. Trainers all over the UK were using it for reactions to cars and joggers and other stimuli. I was even advised via Facebook that Turn and Face works with reactivity to kangaroos too, which really made me giggle. I never even considered that dogs reacted at kangaroos; I've never even seen a kangaroo, yet TAF was helping with kangaroo-reactive dogs in Australia. Another trainer, Sophie Fisher (UK), whose dog I had previously helped with TAF, started to use it as a balancing and calming method, not for a dog, but for a human. She modified it somewhat to use on a dog owner's autistic son, with success!

As all these experienced trainers started to analyse exactly what they were seeing when they witnessed a TAF case transform, they became enthused in their desire to understand and explain it, and TAF started to become something bigger and better than it ever was before.

I had filmed every case that I could for a year, and with the launch of the Turn and Face Instructor Training Scheme, many of the trainers who had initially shown interest joined. There were some very experienced and wise minds scrutinising Turn and Face. I used the case videos to teach all those that wanted to know more. No one was rude, no one was negative, they *all* wanted to understand this and use it to help dogs and owners have better lives. It was a massive highlight in my life. *Finally* I had a keen and wise audience for TAF and *at last* it was finding its way to those that could really help others with it. And with this group of experienced and wise trainers I knew there would be no bricks thrown, only compassion for dogs and their owners, and happiness that they were onto something really new, that could help people and dogs quickly and kindly. I was no longer alone with the 'burden' of TAF.

Then it got better still. I was sent videos of other trainers' TAF assessments and cases for me to give feedback, and so suddenly I was presented with videos of dogs not only from the UK but also from the USA and Australia, so many miles and oceans away. I was watching other people's dogs, being worked under other trainers, from all sorts of places, being helped with TAF. It was an absolute dream come true for me and every day my heart soared when I saw it. I watched dogs benefit from TAF in places around the word that I had dreamt one day I might go to, but which in reality I would probably never see. But TAF was *already there*, even though I was not.

Turn and Face was up and running and there was no stopping it now, and what's more, I was no longer alone with it. It was no longer 'mine'. It belonged to anyone who wanted it to help them, or their clients' dogs. *YES, I had achieved my goal!*

With this new band of TAF instructors on board, there were still mysteries to be understood about why it did what it did. Together with these new minds, we now had the combined knowledge and experience of what amounted to several hundred years of dog ownership and training. Between us, we had experience of many tens of thousands of dogs. As I shared my cases with them by video, we worked together to thoroughly unpick what exactly was going on with TAF. Why was it so successful, so quickly, in so many cases? Using my case studies I shared with them all I could and taught them everything I had learned about Turn and Face. They in turn taught me a bunch of stuff, about both their observations of and experiences with TAF and many other things about dogs that I didn't know. It was a time of great learning and sharing from which we all benefited, and to all those involved I would like to thank you most sincerely for all you have done for TAF and most importantly, for dogs.

Training people using videos seemed to work, so then I decided to make TAF available to anyone at all, not just trainers, in video format. Borrowing more money to do so, I collated a bunch of video case studies of TAF in action with before, during and after footage, and had the DVD professionally recorded and produced and made it available to anyone. I added to this our explanation of why and how TAF works and what causes dogs to become reactive in the first place. The Turn and Face tutorial DVD was up and running, a new website was launched to support and promote it, and TAF was now shared even more widely in the public domain. The heavy burden that TAF had once been was now lifted as it was shared far and wide and proved successful with most dogs.

After a while things began to calm down and the haters started to fade away as they accepted that actually, TAF had not killed any dogs, but instead had saved many of them. Book and DVD sales slowed and had started to become an occasional sale until one day, completely out of the blue, Larry Krohn, another very much followed and well thought-of trainer, posted first about my book being a great book and then later about the Turn and Face DVD and with Larry's public endorsement, another splurge of interest ensued.

★

The timing of Larry's comments could not have been better. They immediately preceded concerns about Connor's health in January 2019. Connor needed a heart scan and the amount of money that was raised via Larry's comments was almost exactly the amount of money I needed for Connor to have the scan. I cannot thank Larry enough for his timely and most fortunate comments in support of the book and DVD. TAF had effectively made Connor's assessment possible. Who could have dreamt of such a thing; TAF has paid me back, by helping my lovely Connor!

As I write this, in February 2019, I have just had someone write to me on Facebook telling me that they have been using TAF. "Several trainers use it round here," she commented. She lives in Oregon. I could not believe that in Oregon, so many miles away, TAF is now routinely in use by multiple trainers. She went on to tell me that TAF had been created by "… a UK trainer called Denise McLeod – you should look her up," she suggested. I pointed out that I was Denise McLeod and we had a good giggle about it.

In the same week, someone else wrote to me thanking me for sharing TAF as it had helped her clients' dogs. Apparently she had heard of TAF on the internet somewhere and then a trainer from Chicago had shown her how to do it. I did not know these people at all, yet TAF was helping them. Also in the same week, a trainer in Scotland, Callum King, had accompanied a client's dog to the vet as the dog was not at all good with vets. He had used TAF to calm the dog to allow the vet to apply a stethoscope to the dog's chest – something that the dog had never allowed before. The vet had been astonished at the sudden drop in heart rate brought about by TAF and asked what the trainer had done to bring it down. This was all unbelievably brilliant news and I remain thrilled every time I hear of such things. I could never have dreamt that it might go so well.

The furore over TAF has died down now. People have grown used to success stories and tales of sudden positive change, and by and large the haters have gone away. I am convinced and thrilled that the original set of trainers who took on TAF as one of their preferred methods are the right people for the job. So many wise and experienced minds. I have always believed that the universe has a way of making things work out, and had I had an opportunity to pick these trainers by hand, then I could not have done a better job than fate itself has achieved without me.

Many people still write to me to thank me for TAF. Many of them wish me luck in the future and hope that it has made me wealthy after the financial struggles I shared with readers in my first book. So for those that want to know – did it make me rich? Nah. At time of writing, I have pretty much recovered my costs and I just have one small loan to pay off. But it has definitely improved the business generally and it has widened my circle of friends.

But best of all, it has made my dream come true – which is worth more than any amount of money – that Turn and Face can go everywhere and help so very many dogs and their owners to live better, happier, calmer and less stressed lives. And there is no doubt at all that it has saved some dogs from being put to sleep through misunderstandings.

In my lifetime I have failed to produce any children, instead I will leave behind a dog-training technique, and in that act I know that I will continue to help dogs and owners long after I am dead and buried. I feel that my purpose on this earth has been achieved and I can rest in peace that I *did* finally find the courage to permanently make a difference to the world of dogs. But I could not have done it without the support of so many wise trainers and friends who helped me and spurred me onwards.

I have always said that if something saves just one dog's life, then any struggle to achieve it has been worthwhile. And there is absolutely no doubt whatsoever that the release of TAF has done that.

I would like to extend a massive thank you to all the trainers, owners, behaviour practitioners, vets, colleagues and friends, who at the beginning made it all happen, and who have supported my first book and Turn and Face and me since the launch. Thank you, and *WE DID IT! We only bloody went and did it! Turn and Face is up and running!*

Finally, when I sit back and look at what has been achieved, I have to say that I am beyond thrilled by the worldwide success of TAF. I am deeply humbled by the support and endorsement of so many great trainers. I was given an accidental understanding of a process so many years ago, and now, more than forty years later, the dog called Ben who started it all has changed the world of dogs forever. Sadly, like any dog-training technique, Turn and Face does not work with every case. I am saddened on the occasions when people write to tell me that Turn and Face has not worked out for them. But for most, it does work to some degree. And for many, it is as fast and effective as it was for Sabre.

★

To the dog that started it all, so very long ago, the dog that taught me Turn and Face. Thank you, Ben! May you rest in the knowledge that your actions have saved and improved lives all over the world. Many dogs are now free of the problems that once bound them, because of you. You live on in the peace and understanding that you have brought to so many. You live also forever in my heart.

Until we meet and walk once more together, run free, sweet boy.

★

For more information about Turn and Face, please go to www. turnandfacereactivedogs.com

Or for general dog training enquiries, please go to www. cadelac.co.uk, my main dog training website, or follow me at CaDeLac Dog Training and Behaviour on Facebook.

Love Is Blind

In the years before I went full-time in dog training, I ran a number of agility classes on a not-for-profit, fun basis. This meant that I could train my own dogs along with those of other people. During this time, I ran classes at four separate venues over a period of several years.

One of these venues was at a kennels and training centre in Leicester, where I met and befriended another trainer who taught obedience there. He was a very knowledgeable man with many years' experience of dog training and handling from his RAF years, and each weekend I would spend valuable time with him, drinking tea and chatting about dogs. There are few things I like more than listening to trainers with more experience than me telling me the stories that have stayed in their heart, and these chats quickly became one of the most enjoyable and educational times of my life. He had experience of dogs working in war zones, dogs doing drug detection, real tracking work, and many other things that I had no experience of, and I was a sponge for anything he said.

Around a year after I met him, he made the decision to buy a whole litter of working-bred Labrador puppies and train them to be drug detection dogs. He got a licence for the drugs, and the training commenced. Week after week I listened to the tales of this week's trips to the railway station, town centre or airport, or I watched as he worked puppy after puppy in the field next to where I trained. He was working hard to socialise and train each puppy individually, and was seemingly doing a good job of it. One day when I asked how things were going he replied, "It's fun, but never again! Properly socialising this number of pups is hard!" He looked so tired. I noted that training a whole litter of puppies up to working standard looked too tiring, and I struck it off my list of possible things to do in the future.

Then one day he came to me as I was setting up agility equipment and asked me if, as a favour, I would mind asking my class to stay behind after their lesson so that he could 'borrow' them to stand in a line-up, in order for his pups, one after the other, to search a line of people for the first time, looking for drugs. He explained, "It's hard to find sufficient numbers of people to stand in a line-up for training purposes. So if they are willing, this would help me and the pups a lot."

He went on to tell me what was required of my agility students, should they take part: "I will give you the drugs to hold and the others will not have drugs. Please explain to your clients what they will be doing, as you might find that some are reluctant to take part in a drugs search." And then he winked at me. I knew what that wink meant.

It was a great set of people who attended that venue. A group of ten worked on the two sets of agility equipment over an hour and a half or so. There were a number of real characters in the group, some new friendships had been formed, several of us had taken to going walking together after class, and a few had started to travel together. There were three men and seven women, and two of these men, Dave and Phil, had struck up a particular friendship and there was much banter and humour between them. They were fun and friendly days where we all got to know one another, not just as dog handlers but as people. On sunny days we often stood chatting and laughing together long after class had finished.

The class came and went without any incident and, as usual, with much laughter, and afterwards we packed away the equipment and people started to hover around chatting, so I made my request.

"Guys, Paul has asked me if any of you would be able to stay behind today and take part in a line-up for his trainee drugs detection dogs to do their first search of multiple humans. The plan is that I will have some drugs on me, and you lot won't, and we just stand there whilst one by one, the pups are brought out to search us all and locate the drugs. Is anyone willing to take part, please?"

As soon as I had said it I saw a number of people shift uncomfortably and begin to look agitated. Phil, the most confident of the whole group, was the first to reply.

"Oh, I'm sorry, but I can't stay today I am afraid as I have to get back home because… er, well, because my wife is having a baby this afternoon."

Dave's head spun sharply toward his friend Phil, and with a look of incredulity on his face he said, "You don't have a wife!"

"Yes I do!" replied Phil defensively.

"Since when?" retorted Dave.

Phil shot Dave a stern look which I presume was meant to silence him and replied, "Since… well, since last weekend!"

Seemingly oblivious to or unfazed by the stern look he had been given, Dave continued to argue with his friend about his alleged marital status as the rest of us looked on with fascination and some humour. "So, you got married last weekend and you're having a baby this weekend? That was quick work!" The usual banter between them continued, but

I detected a growing irritation and unease in Phil. Phil knew that Dave had missed the point of his excuse completely.

"Yes, well that's *why* we got married, because of the baby! It was the right thing to do." Phil was digging a bigger and bigger hole to climb out of.

Also missing the point completely, Dana, a sweet if rather air-headed young girl spoke up, smiling happily. "Oh, how lovely of you Phil. How terribly noble of you!" She smiled again at him somewhat adoringly. Dana, I had long suspected, had a bit of a 'thing' about Phil, but she still seemed happy to hear his news. She continued, "Congratulations! Do you want a boy or a girl?"

Phil turned and just stared blankly at her with his mouth slightly ajar. A look of complete incomprehension and disbelief crept over his face. He failed to answer the question.

Meanwhile Dave, who had still not grasped the real purpose of Phil's excuse to leave, was having none of it. "So, you're telling me that you got married and you didn't tell any of us, *and* you came to agility last week on the same day you supposedly got married, and you still didn't mention it?" Dave still seemed genuinely bemused by his friend's 'baby' story: he just hadn't understood the situation at all.

They had all been standing in a sort of horseshoe shape, shoulder to shoulder facing me as the discussion progressed, but as he spoke these last few words, Phil had stepped out of the line, seemed to raise himself a few inches taller, puff his chest out and turned to face Dave, like he was squaring up for a fight.

"Oh, why don't you just shut up, Dave!" Phil said angrily.

Worried it was all getting out of hand, I called a halt to the proceedings and said, "It's okay to leave if you need to – I know you all have busy lives." Phil looked at me with gratitude in his eyes. Realising that I had understood his excuse a lot better than Dave had, he took the chance I'd just given him, said goodbye and turned to walk away. As he walked he shouted, "Dave, do you still want that lift home? If so, come on, I have to go." Dave wandered off after Phil.

Then Susie spoke up: "I have to go too. I'm a midwife and I promised Phil I'd be on standby for his wife today, *didn't I, Phil?*" She spoke loudly so Phil could hear her.

Phil turned around briefly. "Yes, come on Susie, else you'll be late."

I could have sworn Susie had said she was an accountant just a few weeks ago.

"I have to go too, my in-laws are coming round," said Lisa, turning to leave.

"Yes, mine too," said Fiona.

It seemed it was a day for in-laws visits and baby births. Five of the ten people had now left the field.

I waited until they had all made their escape in their cars and then went to tell Paul that we were ready, but a little down on numbers. The pups came out and most of them did really well. It was fascinating to watch them and see the different approaches each took. Some were methodical, and worked in a slow, consistent way. Others were more hurried and scatty. Some were excited and giddy; others seemed to take it all in their stride. I felt a new fascination for dogs grow in me, and I knew I would have many questions for Paul about what I had seen that day with the pups when I saw him the following week.

Those of us that had stayed enjoyed the activity very much. The process inspired real intrigue in me and though searching for drugs was not an option for my dogs, I began to teach them, and later class dogs, to search for teabags and then their owners' car keys.

★

The following week as people started to arrive for the class I watched as they wandered across the field. Dana was last to arrive and as she did she skipped across the field as if elevated with joy. She looked jolly pleased with herself about something. Dog trotting politely at her side, lead in one hand, she carried a plastic bag in the other. She smiled triumphantly and said hello to everyone, before approaching Phil with an adoring look in her eyes, and passed him the bag.

"Here ya go, Phil," she smiled broadly, "I brought you something!" She beamed from ear to ear as Phil, looking slightly worried, took the bag from her. He held it weakly and slightly away from him, as if he feared the contents.

"Look inside!" she said, her excitement brimming. Phil reached tentatively into the bag and withdrew a beautifully wrapped box-shaped gift, which was all tied up with silver, blue and pink shiny ribbons.

"It's for the baby," she said.

When you get a dog...

In 1994, when my first two dogs, Cassie and Lace, were at the height of their 'fighting stage', I took the decision that when I was asleep, one or other of the dogs was to be shut away in the kitchen, so that they wouldn't start fighting and injure each other whilst I slept. My dogs had always had free access to the house when I was asleep and it saddened me deeply that I had to keep shutting one of them away, but I didn't know how else to keep them both safe.

One morning, I went downstairs and into the kitchen, and as I opened the door I realised immediately that something was very, very wrong with Lace, who had been sleeping there.

Her pretty face was hugely swollen, her eyelids were so puffed up they were almost shut, and her usually delicate little ears were now like tennis balls, rounded and hard, weighing heavily on the side of her head. As I entered the room, she stood and then she tried to raise her head to look up at me, but it seemed too heavy or too painful, so she lowered it again and left it hanging low, just above the ground. Her tail, usually so buoyant when she saw me, hung limply to the ground also. Her top lip was grossly enlarged and billowed above her tooth line. She looked so sad.

My heart jolted painfully in my chest. I felt fear and panic rise in me.

What on earth had happened to her? What could I do?

I stroked her gently, and then quietly telling her to stay and taking Cassie with me to prevent a fight between her and poor Lace, I rushed upstairs, pulled on some clothes, ran back to Lace and picked her up as she seemed reluctant to move. I placed her in the car and drove her straight to the vet. I carried her in my arms into the waiting room and as I entered, I shouted out for help.

The receptionist, seeing Lace's grossly swollen features, leapt to her feet and opening the door behind her, shouted, "Help please, emergency arrival!" Two nurses quickly appeared, closely followed by a vet, and Lace and I were ushered straight into an examination room. The vet asked what had happened whilst he rummaged through a cupboard looking for a syringe and a bottle of something to fill it with. I couldn't offer him any clues as to the cause of this sudden, unsightly swelling. She had been fine the night before, I told him.

Guilt rushed through me as I remembered she'd been locked in the kitchen, all alone, whilst her head, ears and lips had started to swell so badly. She looked so unhappy and uncomfortable. I just hoped she wasn't going to die. I was so shocked at the sight of her.

Lace just stood there, head hanging down. She made no objection at all to the vet gently lifting her lips as he felt the swelling. Normally she hated vets, but this time she didn't seem to care who touched her, or what was done to her. As I held her in my arms, two nurses stood by as the vet checked her over and then on his request, one passed him the syringe he had set to one side.

He told me that he thought she had been stung. He quizzed me: "Have you seen any bees or wasps in the kitchen, dead or alive?" I had not, but then I had not thought to look, I had just got her to the vets as quickly as I could.

He slipped the needle into Lace. She didn't react at all to it. She just stood there looking dreadful.

The vet said he wasn't able to find a sting or the site of a sting, but advised me that he felt almost certain that a sting had been the cause. "Dogs are devils for catching and swallowing bees and wasps," he said, looking at me like the wise man that he was, over the top of his glasses.

And then he gave me the most wonderful piece of advice.

"Denise," he said sagely, "when you get a dog, you need to also buy a lead, a collar, and a packet of antihistamines, which you must carry with you always. Had Lace had an allergic reaction to this incident, she would almost certainly be dead. If this ever happens again, give her an antihistamine tablet immediately. Remember antihistamines can save lives!" He looked sombre and serious and I took on board what he had said.

I'd never even heard of antihistamines until that day. I'd never had cause to see them in action before either, and I was utterly amazed to observe that soon the swelling began to subside, and within a few hours it was completely gone, and Lace's pretty features were once again restored to their former glory.

Lace never slept alone in the kitchen again; in fact, since that day, I have never closed any of my dogs behind a door for any length of time, for a fear of it happening again. I just had to find a way to manage Cassie and Lace's hatred for one another a different way. From that moment forward I trained both dogs to go to their own, separate beds and to stay there, unless I released them. With beds at opposite ends of the room the fighting was prevented for most of the time and I felt able to allow them both into the bedroom with me, trusting them to stay in their personal places on their own beds. Which thankfully at night time at least, they did.

WHEN YOU GET A DOG…

The next day I went out and I bought myself a bum bag, and in it I put two packets of antihistamines that I had bought from the chemist. Since that day, whenever I have a dog with me, I wear my bum bag strapped around my waist. It isn't an attractive look I know, but it is hugely useful and carries also my poo bags, some emergency money and some painkillers. I am now known by some as the 'bum bag' lady. Every so often, I replace them with a new packet even though I have rarely had cause to use them.

★

Over twenty years later, in August 2018, Simon, the dogs and I were touring the beautiful Scottish Highlands and the islands of Skye, Lewis and Harris in our motorhome, on a two-week holiday. The mountains are just awe inspiring, the islands are stunning, the beaches sublime and the people of Scotland some of the most friendly and humorous that I have ever met.

Even the road signs are friendly. 'Please drive courteously' is one that always makes me smile. 'Pull over to allow others to pass' is another. It really works too! People are more courteous on the roads up in Scotland.

We had a fabulous time, but eventually it was time to start the 600-mile journey home. We decided to make the journey over four days to limit the daily driving time, and find parking places to sleep in the van as we went.

After we left beautiful Skye, we drove through the breathtaking Scottish Highlands and after a few hours began to look for somewhere to spend the rest of the evening and night. We found a lovely picnic spot and parked up. Across the car park was another campervan but apart from that, we were alone. We walked the dogs through the heavily wooded terrain and up the hill to see a stunning waterfall, tumbling down, singing as it fell. On the way we picked and ate some wonderful wild Scottish blueberries, then headed back to the van and settled down to sleep. There was some misty rain, but we were safe and dry in the van.

Life doesn't get much better than this!

That fresh, clean Scottish air cleansed one's body and soul, and sleep came easily, to the accompaniment of the gushing river, which rushed by at the bottom of the gully, slightly below us. Everything seemed perfect.

"Aargh! I've been stung!" I woke to the sudden sound and movement as Simon sat up dramatically in bed. He held out his hand to show me what had happened. My eyes were still blurry from sleep, my mind still in a fog of sleepiness. I could see the sting of a bee still pulsating in his hand. "Get some tweezers, get it out," he said. I found the tweezers quickly and removed the sting in its entirety, but he didn't seem relieved; instead he seemed agitated and worried. I later discovered that removing a sting with the side of a credit card or similar, with a single swipe, is a better way. But I didn't know that back then.

Simon is one of those people who usually stays calm, or even becomes calmer, in a crisis. I'm the one who panics and freaks. But he wasn't calm. The sting agitated him immediately. At this stage I thought he was just panicked because it was such a shock and so painful, so soon after being asleep. I tried to calm him. He sent me for the antihistamines and I found them in my bum bag and gave them to him.

Now back sitting on the bed at his side, I picked up my phone to see if I had any Google reception. For the last twelve days we had very rarely had a signal for phone or internet, but thankfully I could see that though I had a very dodgy phone signal, I did have good internet signal and could use Google. So I asked Google what I should do. Some home remedy page recommended I use bicarbonate of soda (for bee stings, not wasp stings). We had located the insect in question and it was a bee, so I covered the area with bicarb and put a bandage on his already-swelling hand, hoping that it would ease the pain and distress.

Then it started to get really scary.

Though it was barely a couple of minutes since the sting had occurred, Simon's other hand had already begun to swell and both of his arms were covered in hives, which appeared to be spreading very rapidly. He said he could now feel tingling in both arms and he asked me to open all the windows – he wanted more air. I noted that although his body had started to go red, his face was now ashen grey and had gone sticky to the touch.

I didn't know what was happening, but Simon did. He had previously had relevant medical training in his army years. He told me to get an ambulance and tell them he was suffering from anaphylactic shock. I'd never heard of it. But I knew I had limited phone reception and not only that, we didn't actually know where we were! How could I get an ambulance with such a dodgy phone signal? Let alone direct an ambulance to us when I didn't know where we had parked. Panic was beginning to rise in me; it was all happening so quickly. I started to shiver in shock.

There was an information sign on the other side of the car park which I had read the previous night, so leaving Simon lying on the bed, I jumped out of the van into the rainy morning and ran to the sign to see if it gave us a clue to our location. The dogs all jumped out behind me and I left the door open, to allow air in.

As I ran, I looked at my phone, praying there was a signal. There was! Five bars! Five glorious bars of signal. As luck would have it, for the first time in twelve nights, we had parked where there *was* a phone signal, at least on this side of the car park.

I dialled 999 and asked for an ambulance. I tried to explain where we were: I knew which road the picnic site was on and I knew roughly how long we had been travelling, and where we had come from and where we were headed.

It began to rain more heavily. I wiped the rain off the information sign with my free arm and began to read the name of the waterfall we had walked to the previous evening. My back was to the van where I had left Simon alone. But still they couldn't locate us. My heart sank so low.

They said they had dispatched an ambulance to Invergarry, the nearest little town to where we thought we were, and told me someone else would ring back immediately with local knowledge. We were just about to hang up when I heard Simon cry out weakly, "Dee". As I spun round to the sound of his voice, I saw him there in the doorway of the van. For a moment he was on his knees, leaning out of it precariously. He was clutching the cupboard with one arm to stabilise himself, but as I started to run towards him, with the phone still to my ear, he slumped forward and fell out of the van and onto the wet car park. He had been searching for more air, but his blood pressure had dropped and he had collapsed at the door. Now he was lying in the rain. I watched his chest heave and fall as he gasped for breath on the wet gravel. He looked utterly dreadful and I noticed his face was beginning to swell.

Panic took me and I screamed down the phone, "He's fallen out of the door, please, *please* help us…"

The call operator said someone would call back immediately, that help was on its way… and that he was going to hang up to allow the other call to come in.

I reached Simon and reassured him that help was coming and sure enough the phone rang again. I answered to the sound of another calm, sensible voice. "After you left the main road that you were on, did you cross a wooden bridge that you drove over before turning right to the car park?"

"Yes, we did, there is a wooden bridge." I squeezed Simon's fingers gently as encouragement.

"Good, I think I know where you are," he said, "I've walked my dog there. Can you get someone to go to the road and wave us down? Is there anyone with you who can help? Tell your husband we are on our way and we will be there very soon. Keep him calm and tell him everything is going to be okay."

For the first time, I felt a glimmer of hope. Hope that my Simon was going to be okay. Things had got so bad so quickly; I was stunned by the speed of events. I told the ambulance driver I would find someone to help us and we hung up.

I turned my attention back to Simon and offered more words of reassurance as the ambulance man had told me to, before leaving him alone once again to bang on the door of the other motorhome parked nearby and pleading with its inhabitants to help us. Bless him, still in his pyjamas, the neighbour came out and helped me cover the rapidly swelling man that I loved with blankets and waterproof coats and gave his head a pillow. The cold Scottish rain was now falling and falling.

Moments later, his wife appeared. She took in the frightening scene before her and following my request, still in her dressing gown, she ignored the cold Scottish rain and ran a quarter mile in the dawn light, back to the main road, to flag down the ambulance.

Simon's chest was heaving as he struggled to fill his lungs with air, his airway was constricting at lightning speed. The colour of his face told its own tale; he looked so very poorly.

Seeing that I too was now sweating and shaking in shock, the kindly man went and put on his kettle, to make me a cup of tea as we waited and hoped that the ambulance would soon come. I talked to Simon and held his hand gently, but felt helpless and wanted to do more, so with my free hand I turned once more to Google for help whilst Simon spent all his energy on drawing air into his lungs.

The words I read sickened me to the core.

Anaphylactic shock is a medical emergency. A severe allergic reaction that can lead to death within 30 minutes. Treatment: Seek medical help immediately. Administer epinephrine/ adrenaline immediately. Do CPR if the person stops breathing.

Death inside thirty minutes? Do CPR if the person stops breathing? But what if you don't have any epinephrine/ adrenaline? What if you are miles away from medical help? Is this for real?

For the first time I realised that there was a distinct possibility that Simon might die here.

We had only been awake for fifteen minutes or so and Simon was now really struggling to breathe. His face was a strange shade of grey and green, like the still pallor of death, as he continued to heave and wheeze air into his lungs. The dogs stood around looking worried and wary, knowing something was seriously amiss, but keeping their distance.

And so we waited. It seemed like we waited for a million years.

And then I heard it. The enormously welcome sound of an ambulance siren in the distance. I so hoped that this was our ambulance. My heart soared as I figured everything would be okay, as long as it got here quickly.

But the welcome sound stopped abruptly, just a few seconds after it had started, and my heart plummeted lower than the rain-covered floor that I sat on.

The kindly man from the van and I had both heard the siren start, then stop. Over Simon's head, he looked at me and I at him; as if of one mind, we both had the same dreadful thought that this was not our ambulance and that the wait might continue for too long... Simultaneously we both started to realise that we might be about to watch Simon die, here, on this car park floor, in this beautiful place.

Oh no! Oh, please no! Don't let him die! The words went round and round in my head as I willed the universe to help us.

My mind flicked forward in horror to a life without Simon. I'd only known him four short years; surely this couldn't be the end, could it? Then it flicked back to the day I met him, the moment he asked if I would marry him, our wedding day, nights we had spent together on lonely moonlit mountains, his lovely smile as he looked out from the balcony on our honeymoon, the laughs we had shared, the love that we felt, spending Christmas laughing with his family, the many miles we had travelled together, the oceans we had crossed and the ancient sights we had seen, standing side by side watching in wonder at stone circles and lines and ancient prehistoric buildings as the dawn sun rose over them, and then as it set again. We had shared so much in such a short time. My mind flicked forward in dread again, to a life without Simon as my stomach twisted and contorted in pain.

I could not allow these thoughts. I brushed them aside and glanced over my shoulder, willing an ambulance to be there, but there was just an empty bridge over a gushing river of beauty. I looked back at Simon; his head had fallen to one side.

I carried on talking to him, but he was no longer talking back now and was starting to look very weak indeed. There was a strange rasping sound coming from his throat. His dog, Cherry, cowering down low to the ground, had crept slowly closer and wanted to be near him. I told her, "Stay there Cherry, it's going to be okay." The last thing he needed was a loving Labrador lying on his chest. Vaguely, I wondered if she knew that he was dying. Do dogs know such things?

I turned to Simon and told him again, "They will soon be here, darling. Hang in there, help will soon be here, it's going to be okay. They are on their way, keep breathing." I noticed my own hand was shaking as I once again took his and bent over to kiss him, but his head had lolled to one side away from me. I noticed that his eyelids were swelling, his swollen bottom lip was beginning to hang down and he had a large lump on the far side of his face. He was staring straight ahead, away from me. His whole head was swelling up. My mind flicked back many years to the day I saw Lace. On that occasion the medics had saved the day, I so hoped that this would end the same way.

And still we waited, as the rain fell and the river gushed and hope began to fade from my heart, to be replaced by sickening terror.

And then I heard a sound over the rushing of the nearby river and as I turned I saw the most beautiful thing I have ever seen: an ambulance. Crossing the wooden bridge it came safely but speedily toward us, soon to be followed by a bedraggled running lady in a dressing gown. Our kindly neighbour, who had given up her sleep to assist a couple of strangers who needed help.

They had arrived!

The ambulance crew came to Simon and together we got him inside the safe haven that is an ambulance, in times of crisis. They asked what had happened, examined the site of the sting, and they injected him with adrenaline.

Relief washed over me as I watched in awe as the wonderfully skilled medics calmly went about checking his vital signs and reassuring him. I watched with such relief as Simon's oxygen levels started to climb on the monitor and his heart began to slow, but then he suddenly started to shake and convulse. I looked up in panic at the medic but he reassured me that it was the effects of the adrenaline. "He is coming back to us – it's going to be okay." He calmed both of us with his words.

Looking back, I don't really know how long it took for the ambulance to get there. We were miles from anywhere, and as it turned out, twenty-five miles from the nearest hospital. But we are so very grateful that it did find us in time.

*

I learned a number of great lessons that day: make sure you know where you are when you lay down your head to sleep, and remember that a phone signal can be a life-saver too!

Simon was taken to hospital where he was given more adrenaline and then stayed on a drip for the next five hours.

He was given several days' worth of antihistamines and steroids, as well as two epinephrine injectors, to be carried at all times and used if necessary. He was given a letter to give to his GP recommending that he underwent allergy tests.

The medical team advised us that symptoms might reappear over the course of the next week, and sure enough, the following day when he awoke, much milder symptoms did start to re-emerge but were alleviated after taking the prescribed tablets.

He remained weak and out of sorts for around five days.

He now carries Epipen injections in a bum bag at all times, as well as a packet of antihistamines.

It is unknown if the antihistamine that I originally gave him had got into his system and begun to at least slow some of the effects of anaphylaxis, but since this event, I have researched and found that it is very likely that it will have helped. I also know now that antihistamine alone will *not* alleviate all of the symptoms of anaphylaxis.

But if the antihistamine did help him, then I find it amazing that a simple piece of advice, given to me about my dog by a vet so many years ago, may have been a contributing factor in Simon's survival.

Good advice is worth sharing!

I would like to state that I am not a medic or a vet in any form and I am not giving medical advice here. But what I do suggest is that you talk to your doctor or pharmacist *and* your vet about the use of antihistamines in both people and animals. From my research at the time of writing, I find that anaphylaxis is on the increase worldwide; it has doubled in the last ten years. I also discovered that whilst some antihistamines (those that make one drowsy) are not recommended for anaphylaxis by all the sites I googled, some are. Luckily the one I carried was. Likewise some brands are not consistently recommended for dogs, but some are. So please find out more from a qualified medic about such a simple, potentially life-saving medicine to assist in the event of you or your animals having a severe, life-threatening reaction.

Simon had had several bee and wasp stings before this event, with only minor swelling and localised pain. The most recent was only five years earlier. But this time, within literally a few minutes, both he and I thought he would die. Recent research has informed me that in fact, people who have been previously stung and not had a reaction are *more* likely to suffer a severe allergic reaction in the future than those who have never been stung before. So surviving a sting is *not* a sign that you will not develop a severe reaction in the future; on the contrary, it makes it more likely that you will!

★

Our deepest gratitude is extended to the two very kind people in the motorhome next door who gave up their sleep and warmth to help us. You were a total gift, thank you so much. The tea was lovely and most welcome. Sorry I didn't have time to wash up my cup.

And heartfelt thanks to every single person involved from the NHS: drivers, medics, doctors, nurses and everyone else who helped that day.

I genuinely believe that the NHS and veterinary teams and all those that work in them are the finest assets of this land that I call home.

THANK YOU FOR DOING THE WORK YOU ALL DO, TO HELP ALL OF US IN NEED AND IN CRISIS!

And huge thanks too to that wonderful vet from years ago; I thank you for your wise words and for possibly saving my husband's life.

"When you get a dog, you also need to get a collar, a lead and a packet of antihistamines that you must carry with you at all times." It seems the same can be applied to when you get a husband.

Let those words live on.

Acknowledgements

Throughout my life I have had ups and downs, highs and lows, joys and deep, disabling sadness, as we all have.

Life is difficult. For all of us. Sometime it is nigh on impossible to see a way out of a hardship or tragedy. Sometimes it throws us curve balls we could not have forsaw. Sometimes it seems impossible to continue. And yet at other times we float on a cloud of seemingly blissful peace.

Throughout all of this, I have been truly blessed with an extraordinary set of friends, neighbors and colleagues who have helped me, supported me, loved me, encouraged me and kept me going. And add to that the fact that I have not one, but now two families loving and supporting me, I consider myself to be one of the luckiest people to be alive. It is time now to give thanks to all of them.

Firstly, to my Mum and Dad, for very generously funding this self published book. Thank you for all you have done for me, particularly in recent times. I could not have published this book without your help. I and many others, will be forever in your debt. Thank you. I love you both dearly. Xx

To my gorgeous husband Simon and his wonderful family, for loving me and supporting me and once again helping me with writing this book as you have. I love you all and am thrilled that you are in my life. Thank you for being you.

To my very dear friend Liz who has supported me and helped me through so much of my life and so many challenges, and for kindly offering to proof read this book before publication. I could not have asked for a better friend than you have been. You are amazing. Thank you.

To my amazing friend Keith Garner, for continuing to be there for me, in the good, the bad and the ugly days. You are a true and wonderful friend for all time. Your kindness and love will never be forgotten. Remember always, you too are loved! Never forget it.

To the brilliant team at CaDeLac, for putting up with me, covering for me and helping me as you have over the years through all that we have shared together. To Annie, Sue, Charlie, Adrian, Allan, Emily and Gill I give thanks for all you do to help me and the dogs and owners that we meet through CaDeLac. You are all amazing and none of what we achieve would be possible without you. Thank you dear friends.

To my special friend Andrew, for helping me out with CaDeLac when things got tough and for being there, ever patient ever peaceful and ever giving. I will always remember your kindness. Thank you.

To some amazing friends Dave, Holly and Holly's Mum Eileen, for helping me and giving me refuge during the worst of times, especially through the difficult 'van years'. I give thanks for our friendship and may light and love bless you always as you have blessed my life.

To John Harding for your years of love and friendship, and for being there on some of the most difficult days of my life, the passing of both Lace and Cloud. Your strength was invaluable and I will always be in your debt. Live long and stay strong my dear friend.

To Sophie Fisher and her team from Max Dogs, for taking care of Karma and Cherry whilst I took care of Connor when he was so poorly. And for being an amazing friend and source of support and sanity, thank you Sophie.

To Wendy and John Brookes, for being brilliant friends and supporters of me and Turn and Face and for providing me with the use of the very first ever video footage of Turn and Face, and endless support ever since. And of course to the lovely Polo, one of my favourite ever TAF case dogs.

To Jean for our walks and talks and for straightening me out on more than one occasion, I give thanks for our special friendship. Love always to you.

To my neighbor Louise for helping me and being there for me time and time again, but mostly for helping me lift Connor when he was so very poorly. Your kindness will always be remembered. Connor loves you too.

And to my other neighbours, Brandon, Di, Paul and Andy, who have helped me, been kind to me and been there for me, Thank you. It is an amazing place to live, made all the better for your being there.

To the friends of old who have now left my life. I thank you for all that we shared, for all that you gave me and for all that you were to me. You will remain as you were, still a friend, in my heart, until its last beat has passed.

To the superbly brilliant trainer and friend Martha Hoffman, my dear friend and trainer Gareth Rees, the very talented trainer and friend Andy Lea (Dogman Downunder), the highly inspirational trainer and friend Sharon Nelson, my old mate and trainer Dave Blackshaw, a treasured friend and trainer Sophie Fisher, the talented US trainer Trish Wamsatt and the amazing trainer Adrianne Beattie who have been in support of and users of Turn and Face right from the very beginning. I cannot thank you all enough. Not just for your support of Turn and Face, but also for your support of me, my first book and our friendship. Thank you so very much for all that you have done and continue to do, for dogs and their humans.

And to the amazing talented trainer Larry Krohn and trainers Denys White, Sarah Whitely, Michael Emans, Callum King, Bob Decker, Bev Broughton, Trish Mitchell, Elizabeth Simpson, Dianne Sanlorenzo, Charlie Reading, Becky Woodruff, Lesley Short, Julie Bond, Jessica Torrence, Rosemary Mortimer, Jo Moor, Jamie Robinson and Jennifer Phillips.

A special thank you to Jackie Fraser for your kind support and help during some tough times, when I wondered which way to turn.

And many others who have taught, used, supported, promoted, or helped me with Turn and Face along the way. Each of you has played a part in changing the world of dogs forever and for saving some dogs lives! I thank you all from the bottom of my heart.

An additional special thank you to inspirational trainer Larry Krohn, for 'accidentally' raising enough money for my Connors heart scan. I can not thank you enough for your timely generosity of spirit by talking so publicly and kindly of Turn and Face and my book.

To Sarah Smith of Charwell Proof Plus Proofreading. Thank you for turning my original ramblings into readable sense, for your encouraging words and support and for your friendship. You are amazing please stay that way!

Thanks also must go to the whole team at Matador publishing for your patience, timeliness, and professionalism throughout the whole publishing process.

To Emma, and all the vets, Nurses, and receptionists at STAR veterinary practice for unparalleled service and veterinary care for all three of my dogs, especially during Connors worst time. I have never before encountered a veterinary practice like yours. Your standards of patient and client care are, I believe, unparalleled and your animal handling skills second to none. Thank you for all you did for Connor and me during those terrible first few weeks.

With heartfelt thanks to those that have provided me with wonderful photographic memories of my dogs – I thank you all.

To Matt Malyan for the stunning front cover image, the picture of Bruce and the gang, and the internal photo of Cloud's beautiful head, Linda Shearman for the brilliant back cover photo of the dogs and I. Michelle Law for the picture of Cloud trotting. Alan Crich for the pictures of puppy Cloud. Thomas Longton for the picture of Cloud working sheep. Simon Brown for the photo of Connor In the sea. Andy at The Working Sheepdog website for the stunning picture of Connor working sheep Paul with Patch for the picture of Connor competing in obedience. Dave Blackshaw for the picture of Cassie jumping. Nikki at Barefoot Photography for the wedding photo. And to the owners of the other stars of the book, Ace, Cooper and Bruce for your respective photos of your amazing dogs.

I also give a very special thank you to the breeders of the puppies I have owned, Cloud, Connor and Karma, namely Sarah McGill, Ruth Morris and Andy Nickless/Gill, for allowing me to have the pleasure of owning and loving your brilliantly produced pups . I owe you a debt for all time.

But most of all I would like to thank my very own special dogs, Cassie, Lace, Cloud and Mirk who taught me so much and gave me so much but who have sadly crossed the rainbow bridge. You live in my heart for all time and I hope that one day we will meet and walk together again. Until then, Run free and have fun. I love you and I miss you so much it still hurts. To my gorgeous boy Connor, Crazy Karma and ever loving Cherry who are still at my side, thank you for teaching me and helping me to love life in the way that you do. For wagging your tails when you see me and for sharing your own dog wisdom with me.

There are few worse feelings than forgetting to thank a special person for their help, as I did in the first book. Sorry to those affected. I am quite certain that I will have forgotten someone else, here in this book, so I apologise in advance for that too. But if you have ever helped me, befriended me, supported me, or been kind to me, my dogs or Turn and Face, then I thank you.

And finally, I would like to thank you, the readers, for giving me an opportunity to relive some of the most special times of my life, for remembering my dogs who have walked the rainbow bridge without me, and for remembering again, some of the wonderful people and dogs that have taught me, helped me, or inspired me.

May the love of a dog, fill your heart for all time.

Love and light to you all.

Denise xx